In
The
Process

4:34

BEN OWDEN

IN

THE

PROCESS.

Where God prepares you for your destiny

Ben Owden is a storyteller and preacher.

IN THE PROCESS
PUBLISHED BY PISTIS
www.pistis434.com

26 25 24 23 22 21 20 19 18   1 2 3 4 5 6 7 8

Hardcover ISBN 978-9987-878-01-7
Paperback ISBN 978-9987-878-00-0
eBook ISBN 978-9987-878-02-4
Audio Book ISBN 978-9987-878-03-1

Edited by Christina and Edith Bwana. The interior design and layout done by Christopher Bupe. Cover design by Jun Nakatsugawa, Illustration by Edgar Lushaju and Author photograph by Alpha Johnson.

SPECIAL SALES
All Pistis books are available at special quantity discounts when purchased in bulk by corporations, organizations, and special-interest groups. For information, please e-mail talktome@benowden.com

To

Tina Stefania

And the love, faith and hope you spread.

Contents

PREFACE   1

PROLOGUE: Introspect   3

Act 1
The In Between

1 Can We Skip This Part?   9

2 What Exactly is Faith?   17

3 The Right View of the Process   31

4 The Process Affords Us Ultimate Worship   41

Act 2
Built for Impact

5 Dust off the Painting   51

6 Modeled for Us and Commissioned to Us   57

7 A Character Built for Impact   63

Act 3
The Prize of the Process

8 Conformity to Christlikeness   75

9 Complete Joy For The Christ-like   89

Act 4
The Great Discourage- ment

10 The Great Discouragement   103

11 The Lie of the Enemy   107

12 Functioning Perspective   115

13 The Great Encouragement   123

Act 5
The Internship for Your Destiny

14 The Full Picture God   133

15 Character Based Destiny   139

16 We Don't Get the Memo   149

17 Faithful Stewardship   155

Act 6
The Greatest Job of All Time

18 Mission Focused Ambition   165

EPILOGUE: The Call to Shape Culture   177

ACKNOWLEDGEMENT   187

ABBREVIATIONS   191

NOTES   193

Preface

What comes to mind when you hear the words "in the process"? The different things that are rushing through your mind right now are most definitely vast and maybe even overwhelming. No one human being is strange to the concept and reality of the process. We all go through it. We have all been through it. We are all going through it.

I didn't write this book to address the general concept of a process. I wrote this book to address a specific process. A process not all, but some choose to go through. The some I am talking about are the people who are tired of the status quo, people who have decided to live for something bigger than themselves, those who dream God sized dreams, and those who live purposeful lives, the ones who have stepped into their calling. This is the group of people I had in mind when writing this book.

Majority of the people with God sized dreams live short of their potential because they don't know how to walk through the process. They don't have the right knowledge of the process to walk faithfully in it in a way that gets them to where God wants them to go. This book aims at equipping you with the right knowledge of the process so that before you meet the Lord you get to say, I have fought the good fight, I have finished the race, I have kept the faith. Now, I do not claim to have covered everything in this book. This book is just another addition to the process canon, and I owe a great deal to those who have done a wonderful job of educating us about the process.

I wrote this book to individuals who have received Christ Jesus as their Lord and Savior, namely Christians. These are the people I am addressing throughout the book. It is important to keep this in perspective so that you don't take anything written in this book out of context. The people addressed in this book are those who are justified by grace through faith and faith alone. People who are already in a relationship with God, who have received the gift of the Holy Spirit, people who are fully sons and daughters of God, people who live in the abundance of the grace of God and the riches of His mercy.

As you read this book, please remember that you are already saved by grace through faith alone. You are already in Christ and He is in you. Works will not get you saved.

As I also mentioned before, this book is primarily written for people who have been called by God into different areas and have decided to step into their calling, people who know God's purpose for their lives and those who dream God sized dreams. This is not to say that the principles of this book don't apply to other areas of life, some of them do, so even if you're not the primary audience of this book, I still urge you to read this book, I am sure you will receive something useful.

It's my prayer that this book challenges, changes and shapes your view of the process. And it's my prayer that the applied truth of this book equips you to finish your race.

Ben Owden

Prologue

I want you to be brutally honest with yourself. Why do you do what you do? Why do you live for what you live for? Why do you have faith in God? Why do you have big dreams? Why do you pursue what you are pursuing? Why aren't you pursuing what you are called to pursue? Why do you pray? Why don't you pray? Why do you read the Bible? Why don't you read the Bible?

The day I decided to be brutally honest with myself and asked myself these questions, I came to a painful conclusion. I am selfish. More than I cared to discover. It all trickled down to me. It all came down to self. I wanted to be successful to prove to people that I made the right choice to go into ministry. I am not a failure. Faith was just a means to get what I want from God, and relationship with God was not on top of that list. I was pursuing God's purpose for my life because I wanted to feel like I matter. I wanted to make a name for myself, to be remembered, to leave a legacy. It was for my own ego boost. That's honesty for you.

Now on the surface it looks like I am doing all the right things, right? You might even be thinking, "This is a guy who's got it all together." I mean, I've got faith in God, and I am faithfully serving at my local church. I am hungry for success and I am pursuing God's purpose for my life. Isn't this the dream for most of us? I mean in this generation, if you aren't all about purpose, calling and big dreams, what are you living for? Let me borrow words from Mark Batterson and Malcolm Gladwell: *If you are not a lion chaser and an outlier, who are you?*

But have you ever stopped to ask yourself why? Why do you pursue your purpose? Why do you do what you do?

It's easy to fall into the trap of doing the right things for the wrong reasons. What are your intentions for doing what you do? Why did you decide to read this book?

You may be wondering, "Something is utterly wrong with you, Ben; you call making decisions that are good for you, selfish? I call that common sense."

You can already see how we see and perceive things differently. All this depends on what we use to draw the nub for our worldview. The basis for your worldview produces your worldview. Which produces your beliefs, which then creates your values and your values produces your behavior. And ultimately it produces your whole life experience.

Today alot of Christians are conflicted. Most of us have ceased to use the Bible as the basis for our worldview. We have resorted to pop culture and public popular opinion and facts. Yet we expect to become unstoppable Christians. It's ludicrous. Let me explain. This is a generation that lives with the mantra "We are living in a fast lane, life is short so go get yours." We approach almost everything with this broken mindset. Time is not on our hands, and because patience is not a common virtue, we do what's good for us. We lean on what seems to be working in the now. We are all about our agenda. For a long time I was a prisoner of this broken, distorted, unbiblical, perverted and unchristian worldview. Everything was a means to benefit me. It was all about me. On the surface, I was doing all the right things (to subconsciously benefit the "me" agenda). This was my inner core. Doing all the right things, for the wrong reasons.

THE DISCERNER OF THE HEART

This deceptive inner core is a common dysfunction for most of us. God Himself said, "*The human heart is the most deceitful of all things, and desperately wicked. Who really knows how bad it is?*" (Jeremiah 17:9, NLT). We are at a risk of living our whole lives doing the right things for the wrong reasons. Wasting our lives. Forgetting that God cares more about the intention than the act itself. Thankfully, He gave us a tool that can discern our deceitful hearts. But it's going to require us taking a brutally honest look inside the depths of our hearts.

The Bible says: "...Blessed is the one...whose delight is in the law of the LORD, and who meditates on his law day and night. That person is like a tree planted by streams of water, which yields its fruit in season and whose leaf does not wither— whatever they do prospers" (Psalm 1:2-3, NIV).

Notice here how the meditation of the Word is what produces fruit. The meditation of the Word of God is directly compared to a stream of water. The fruit is the result of what's happening inside the plant. What's happening inside the plant is the result of the stream of water beside it. I don't know if you're catching this. The Word also says: "For the Word of God *is* living and powerful, and sharper than any two-edged Word, piercing even to the division of soul and spirit, and of joints and marrow, and is a *discerner of the thoughts and intents of the heart*" (Hebrews 4:12).

There we have it. Even though the heart is deceitful above all things, the Word of God is the only thing that can discern its intentions and motives. This only happens when we use the Word of God to do real introspection, in real time, all the time. Only the Word of God is able to call out your heart and strip it naked. His Word says, "He sent His Word, and healed them, and delivered them from their destructions" (Psalm 107:20, KJV). The Word of God alone can blatantly expose the buried and hidden intentions of your heart.

WHY DO YOU DO WHAT YOU DO?

Before we go any further I want you to do a brutally honest self-diagnosis of your heart. For this book to have impact in your life your heart can't be playing deceiver Knievel. By the grace of God this book has the potential of changing your worldview of the process and ultimately your life. But your heart needs to have good soil for this book to bear fruit in your life.

the in between the
in between **the in be-
tween** the in between
the in between the
in between **the in be-
tween** the in between
the in between the in
between **the in be-
tween** the in be-
tween **the in
between** the
in between

the in between
the in between **the in
between** the in be-
tween **the in between**
the in between **the in
between** the in be-
tween **the in between**
the in between **the in
between** the in betwe

01

Can we skip this part?

I often ask myself, why do we hate the process so much? I mean, there's just something about the process that's not appealing to us. We love the calling, we love the dream, we love the promise and we love the manifestation. But ooh boy, we hate the process. Most of us have cried out to God many times, "Can we skip this part, please?"

So what is this process that we so dread to go through? Generally, a process is a series of actions or steps one takes in order to achieve a particular end. This means everything in this life has a process. Before a baby sees the light of day s/he spends nine months inside the womb. Before a cake can even begin to taste good, it spends time in the oven. An elephant's baby stays in the womb for ninety five weeks while a human baby stays in the womb for about forty weeks. If you want to harvest tea it will take you at least three years to get a plant that will produce enough leaves to make a harvest while it takes seven to nine months to harvest coffee. So everything has a process but the duration of each process is different.

Even though God has designed processes like forty weeks pregnancies and ninety five weeks pregnancies, the duration of each process in this life isn't as fixed nor is it written on stone. A good example is my little sister who stayed in our mother's womb for fifty two weeks instead of forty weeks. Another good example is how long you have been waiting for God to answer that big prayer of yours.

Going through the process is the principle of life. It applies to everyone on earth. No one is exempted from the process. There's a process to how our brains develop, how we develop different habits and how we form and discover who we are. Although the process of self-discovery is a very popular subject right now, this book is not about that.

When we read the Bible, we first come to an understanding of who God is, how powerful, how sovereign, how good and how loving He is. We come across many promises of blessings from God. He promises purpose, provision, protection, and salvation for our families, He promises healing, and victory and on and on. We also come across who God says we are and why we were created. We learn that God has a purpose for each one of us. We learn that God dares us to believe Him for the impossible. In Mark Batterson's words, we learn that, "Jesus didn't die just to keep you safe. He died to make you dangerous"

To unlock these promises of purpose and a supernatural life, we learn that we need to pray to God. And pray in the name of Jesus. Believing without a doubt that God will deliver and boom, they are ours. But between these God spoken promises, God given dreams, God's call on our lives, our big bold prayers and their manifestation stands the annoying and unwanted process also known as the "waiting period." A period most of us don't really enjoy. A period most of us want to skip but a period we all must go through.

God is holding the remote and He never skips this part.

This book is about the life that happens in this in-between period. So buckle up, it's going to be one heaven of a ride.

I welcome you to join me in this adventure of understanding and unpacking what the process is and why it's in our best interest to go through it. I will be using the words the-in-between, the waiting and the process interchangeably to refer to the core theme of this book, that is; the life that happens between the dream-the call-the promise-the prayer and the manifestation-the destiny.

WHAT AM I SUPPOSED TO DO NOW?

Every single believer in the world is living in the process right now. This statement is true at any given hour of any given day of any given year, till the end of time. If you are not in the process, you belong to the grave. In this moment right now, you are waiting for something you are believing God for. Something He has called you into, a God given big scary dream. The amazing fact of life here is that, the process doesn't end when God manifests His answers to you, because just as one process ends, another one begins. We will always be in the process because most of life, if not all of it, happens in the process. It is a shockingly beautiful fact of life.

You might be in the process waiting on God to open doors to manifest your dreams. You might be in the process waiting on God to manifest your calling. You might be in the process to experience the full manifestation of what you have been believing God for. You might be waiting for your dream job. You might be in the process waiting for healing. You might be in the process waiting for God to bless your marriage with a child. You might be in the process waiting for victory over the giants that have kept you captive for a long time. You might be in the process waiting for God to deliver you from what's been holding you back. You might be in the process waiting for God to save your marriage. You might be in the process waiting for the right one. You might be in the process waiting for your business or your product to blow up. You might be in the process waiting for God to redeem your family, friends, spouse or children. The truth is, we are all in the process waiting on God to manifest answers to our prayers or His promises to us. While this book will heavily focus on the process pertaining to our big bold dreams and God's call on our lives, the principles in this book apply to whatever you're waiting God for. So keep on reading.

The problem begins with our worldview. Patience is not a common virtue. To make matters worse, over time we have become the ETA generation. Technology has afforded us the ability to know the Estimated Time of Arrival for a lot of the things we do. A microwave, washing machines, downloads, GPS systems, Ubers, machines and software applications all have timers. In this generation we have the ability to know how long what activities will take. And because of this we've become more accustomed to certainty. We passionately love certainty. It's this love for certainty that makes us hate the process we have to go through after we pray and believe God for the big dreams, after we step out to pursue God's call on our lives, after we believe God for the impossible. God doesn't grace us with an ETA or a timer. It's all in His terms and His time. It's all about faith.

THE BIG MOMENT OF FAITH

We usually get super excited and pumped up when we first hear a promise from God or read of His promises from His Word. The day we discover our purpose and calling. The day we decide to chase our dreams. When we read books both Christian and secular that cover subjects about bold faith, big dreams and purpose.

When we read the story of David defeating Goliath with a slingshot, and learn how we can overcome our giants and obstacles. How we can conquer our fears and become unstoppable. How we are victorious in, with, and through our Lord Christ Jesus.

When we read about how God used what was in the hands of Moses to unleash God's call on his life. Accomplishing great things like parting the red sea. We get excited about how God will use what's in our hands to unleash His call on our lives. And how He will accomplish greater things for His glory.

We get super excited because if God accomplished so much in the OT (Old Testament) times when Christ was not fully revealed, what is He going to do now that we have a better covenant? Now that we have been given the Name above all Names to seal our prayers with. Now that we have His Holy Spirit living in us and praying to God for us. I mean, this is the Spirit of God, so life can't get any better than this...right?

This is the take back era

This is the era of dominion

This is the believe big or go home era

We get on our knees and pray to God for things. We believe God for the impossible. We believe God to manifest our big audacious dreams. We believe God for the immeasurably more than what we ask or imagine. We declare some things and because we know and believe God to be faithful, so the intensity of the excitement of this moment is REALLY BIG! Our faith experiences an adrenaline rush.

Because hey!

My God is not a small God,

He is mighty and big!

He is powerful and able!

He is sovereign and faithful!

He is the same yesterday, today and forever!

He will come through for me the way He did;

David, Moses, Joshua, Daniel and Abraham.

This excitement grows bigger the more we anticipate God's manifestation. But between the promise, the dream, the calling, the prayer and the manifestation of the answer, stands the process-the in-between-the waiting and boy, we just wish we'd get rid of this stage. We become consumed with the excitement of the manifestation that we just want to skip the process, who likes that in-between anyways, right? Just as how you want to skip this repetitive part of the book and jump to the real stuff, right? Instead of perceiving the process as a beautiful and an enjoyable part of life, we perceive it as a buzz killer.

THE HEROES WE LOOK UP TO

As you study the Bible, you begin to realize all the people we admire and look-up-to; the heroes of faith who have inspired many generations, all had to go through the process. People like Joseph, who spent 13 years between the dream and Him living out the dream. People like Abraham, who spent 25 years being in the process waiting for Isaac. David, who spent years in the process after he was already ordained to be a king by Samuel.

When you look into the lives of the Faith warriors in the Bible; you begin to see a waiting pattern. They all had to go through the process just like you and I. The process was an essential part they had to go through before God manifested His promises to them. This realization stirs up more serious questions, like, why does God take us through the process? Why is the process important to God? Why should the process be important to me? How should I go through the process?

The remainder of this book will unpack this message.

THE FATHER OF FAITH WAS NOT SPARED

Abraham is an extremely famous guy. He is probably the most blessed person in the whole Bible. God blessed Abraham and his descendants abundantly. In fact, Jesus was born through his lineage. To the end of time, through Abraham, all families on the earth will be blessed. But everything we know about Abraham's legacy started with a promise.

Abraham was 75 years old when God called him out of his hometown called Ur of Chaldeans to a land that God will show him. This calling came with a promise. We read about this in Genesis, "Now the Lord had said to Abram, Get out of your country, from your family and from your father's house, to a land that I will show you. I will make you a great nation, I will bless you and make your name great; and you shall be a blessing." (12:1-2).

Imagine how amazing and exciting it must have been for Abraham to hear this from God. He must have spent his youth hearing about how God spoke to his ancestor Noah. How God told Noah to build an ark and even though everyone thought he was bonkers, God eventually manifested what He promised. The same God is now launching a new mission with Abraham. Abraham must have been super excited for getting such a fresh start at age 75. And not just a fresh start, this was a grand start. People were probably spreading nasty rumors about Sarah's barren womb. He probably thought his nephew Lot was going to be the only son he will ever have. Then God shows up and says, "I will make you a great nation." God doesn't say I will make you a great family. He says, "I will make you a great nation." I can picture Abraham and Sarah so excited; preparing for the move. This moment must have been overwhelming. And a lot of us can relate to this moment, the moment of the promise, the moment of the big bold prayers, the moment of bold faith, the moment of the big move. The moment God calls you. The excitement of this moment is colossal.

Following the pinnacle of that excitement was the process. We know that the manifestation of the promise happened twenty five years after the promise, at least part of it. To this day every time a person believes in Jesus and receives the gift of eternal life, it becomes an exclamation mark on God's promise to Abraham when He said through Him all families of the earth will be blessed.

Abraham and Sarah spent twenty five long years in this waiting period. They hit their lowest when Sarah convinced Abraham to sleep with the maid. Also known as taking matters into your own hands. A choice the majority of us make when we are in the process. This absurd choice didn't move, skip or rush God at all in the process He was taking Abraham through. At His perfect time He opened Sarah's womb. This perfect time happened to be twenty five years after the promise.

We all go through the process. No one escapes it. There are no exceptions to this principle. Without faith, the process can't be completed. Without the process, faith wouldn't be required. And without faith, we are simply godless creatures.

02

What exactly is faith?

The Word of God says: "But without faith it is impossible to please Him, for he who comes to God must believe that He is, and that He is a rewarder of those who diligently seek Him." (Hebrews 11:6) And the Word of God defines faith as "the substance of things hoped for, the evidence of things not seen." (Hebrews 11:1). The Bible also says: "For we walk by faith, not by sight." (2 Corinthians 5:7).

This means, it is only possible to please God when we have faith. Now, expanding this with the two scriptures, it is only possible to please God when we fully believe Him for things that are not yet in front of us. This means, the only possible way to please God is to fully trust that He will do what He has promised to do. I am building something here, so bear with me.

The Word also says for we walk by faith not by sight. So piecing this together; "For we live our lives by fully believing that God is who He says He is and He will do exactly what He says He will do." We don't live by believing

God through what our eyes can already see.

To say this in a different way would be; the only possible way to please God is by living your life fully believing that God is who He says He is and He will do exactly what He says He will do, and not believing Him on the merit of what you already see. Simply put, *faith is taking God at His Word.*

I hope this definition challenges your definition of faith. I know it challenged me. Faith is like the air we breathe. You don't just need air when you go to work or when you need to get something done, you need air all the time to stay alive. You need air in good days and bad days. In the same manner we need faith. Faith is being in a constant state of believing God and His Word regardless of circumstance and time.

WHAT ABOUT US?

After defining faith, the next big question becomes, what about you and me? Where does this definition of faith leave us? I mean, some of us are taught that faith includes believing who and what God says I am, but I don't see it in the above definition. This is a good question to ask. Believing who and what God says you are is covered in the above definition of faith.

In the previous subchapter I defined faith as simply taking God at His Word. While His Word covers who He is and what He will do, it also covers who and what He says you are. So taking God at His Word also includes you believing who and what He says you are. Let me take this deeper. The expanded version of the definition says, faith is believing that God is who He says He is and He will do what He says He will do. Who is God? Among many things, He is the truth, everything He says is true. Let me explain. God is the truth, and only truth comes out of His mouth, which means His Word is altogether true, every part of it. And His Word says a lot about who you are and what you are. So in reality, when you believe Who God says He is, you are also believing who He says you are because if He is true then what He says about you is also true. These two things aren't separate. They are one. If you believe God, then you'll believe what He says about everything, including you. Throughout the course of this book, I will use the expanded definition of faith, but please keep in mind that what He says about everything, including you is part of that definition.

THE TESTIMONY OF FAITH

In the popular faith hall of fame we read in Hebrews 11, we find a character most of us know for the fact that he didn't die but God raptured him, Enoch. We first read about Enoch in Genesis, "And Enoch walked with God; and he was not, for God took him." (5:24). We then read in the New Testament that: "For we walk by faith, not by sight." (2 Corinthians 5:7). This means that Enoch walked by faith, not by sight. In simple terms, Enoch lived his life by fully believing that God is who He says He is and He will do exactly what He says He will do. We also read in Hebrews, "By faith Enoch was taken away so that he did not see death, "and was not found, because God had taken him"; for before he was taken he had this testimony, *that he pleased God. But without faith it is impossible to please Him,* for he who comes to God must believe that He is, and *that* He is a rewarder of those who diligently seek Him." (11:5-6). Scriptures continue to show us that Enoch's testimony was that he pleased God. In fact, these verses in Hebrew only confirm what was written in Genesis; that *Enoch walked with God.* He walked by faith and not by sight. His testimony was faith; Enoch took God at His Word. This is the whole essence of faith, regardless of our circumstances.

FAITH IS A COVENANT

Faith is what gives you the audacity to ask God for the impossible, to dream big and to step into your calling. Faith is what gives you the boldness to ask God for the impossible, be it believing God for a miracle, for provision, for your dreams, your business, for a job or a child. Whatever it might be, it is faith that gives you the boldness to step out and believe God for something out of your reach. This audacity is simply living your life by taking God at His Word.

Faith is not initiated when we pray to God; faith is birthed when we hear the Word of God. The more we know God, the more our faith grows. The more we know His Word, the more our faith grows because faith is simply taking God at His Word. Without His Word we have no basis for our faith.

Faith is living our everyday lives believing in God. Sadly we live our lives by believing God situation by situation. Faith has become the jet to transport us to our dreams. Flying us into our callings. Faith has become a means to solve our problems. Instead of being the means to a relationship with a God who yearns to be intimate with us. There are two groups of situation-by-situation faith. One group is well versed in the Word of God but crippled with unbelief and the second group is simply ignorant of the Word of God. Both groups miss out on the fullness of what faith really is.

Faith has neither a deadline nor an expiry date. Faith isn't initiated when we pray; faith is displayed when we pray. When we live our daily lives by simply taking God at His Word, prayer and declaration become an act of worship. Faith is saying God, You are who You say You are, and I am not going to tie your goodness to my lack of patience. Faith is the life lived with the focus placed on Jesus, ALL THE TIME. This focus is magnified in the process. But this focus doesn't end at manifestation. Faith has neither a deadline nor an expiry date.

Faith is a covenant. It should not be broken by circumstance. No one has modeled faith better than Jesus. To Jesus, faith is a covenant. No circumstance affected His faith. He took God at His Word ALL THE TIME. We are called to be like Jesus.

Marriage is a covenant joining man and woman to become one.

Faith is covenant joining God and man to become one.

God's vows in this covenant relationship are found in His Word, the Bible. Below is an excerpt of His vows in this marriage.

...I will fight for you, be still...

...Do not fear, for I am with you; do not be dismayed, for I am your God...

...I will strengthen you and help you; uphold you with my righteous right hand...

...When you pass through the waters, I will be with you; and when you pass through the rivers, they will not sweep over you...

...When you walk through the fire, you will not be burned; the flames will not set you ablaze...

...Though the mountains be shaken and the hills be removed, yet my unfailing love for you will not be shaken nor my covenant of peace be removed...

...No weapon formed against you will prevail, and you will refute every tongue that accuses you...

...For I know the plans I have you, plans to prosper you and not harm you, plans to give you hope and a future...

...I tell you, whatever you ask for in prayer, believe that you have received it, and it will be yours...

...take delight in the LORD, and He will give you the desires of your heart...

...and call on me in the day of trouble; I will deliver you, and you will honor me...

...If you declare with your mouth, "Jesus is Lord," and believe in your heart that God raised Him from the dead, you will be saved...

...The Lord is a refuge for the oppressed, a stronghold in times of trouble...

...Do not be anxious about anything, but in every situation, by prayer and petition, with thanksgiving, present your requests to God. And the peace of God, which transcends all understanding, will guard your hearts and your minds...

...Trust in the Lord with all your heart and lean not on your own understanding; in all your ways submit to Him, and He will make your paths straight...

...And I will do whatever you ask in my name, so that the Father may be glorified in the Son. You may ask me for anything in my name, and I will do it...

...If you love me, keep my commandments...

...Ask and it will given to you; seek and you will find; knock and the door will be opened...

...I am the way, the truth and the life. No one comes to the Father except through Me...

Your vow in this covenant relationship with God is a one liner, "I believe you Lord God."

Before you doubt Him remember His vows to you in His covenant relationship. Remember His character. God never breaks a covenant nor a vow.

He is faithful

He never changes

His Word is ever true

What He says He will do

The Word of God is not only life. They are God's vows in a covenant relationship with you. God never breaks a covenant. This covenant is your security. Faith is a covenant joining God and you to become one. Faith is about relationship first. Everything else flows from this relationship. Dreams and callings are secondary to relationship.

THE LOVE LANGUAGES OF GOD

Like in any relationship, it's important to learn the love language of the person you are in a relationship with. In this case, it's paramount for you to learn God's love languages. He probably has many love languages, but I will talk about two love languages that have been revealed to me.

The first one is faith, which we have already covered at length, and which we will continue to talk about throughout this book. Yes, faith is an expression of your love for God. Like we have seen before, it's the kind that pleases Him, the kind that gives Him pleasure. It's the second love language, which is a fruit of the first, that I want to touch on here.

Obedience

For a long time, I always thought obedience is this ridiculous unrealistic expectation that God has set upon us. I couldn't live up to it. I felt like Paul who said, "I do not understand what I do. For what I want to do I do not do, but what I hate I do." (Romans 7:15, NIV) Obedience felt like a trap. Even though I wanted to obey, I failed. And when I failed, I condemned myself. I wasn't alone in this; I also saw the attempts of many people fail miserably. I later came to realize that I was looking at obedience without the cross. And the minute I started looking at obedience through the lens of the cross, I started to see how beautiful obedience is.

Jesus said, "If you love Me, keep my commandments." (John 14:15, NIV). When Jesus was telling this to His disciples, He wasn't giving them absurd conditions or unrealistic expectations. He was revealing His love language. Basically saying, if you want to show you love me, obey what I have taught you. So obedience is the expression of our love for God, and this expression is a fruit of faith. You believe first, then, you are able to obey. That's why you get saved before you begin to obey. Your obedience doesn't give you salvation, it's in Christ's obedience that you were saved. So no one can boast in their obedience.

Let me say it in another way. In the previous subchapter, I've talked about how faith is a covenant and in this covenant God is the one who first pursues us. He is the one who makes the promises, He is the one who tells us who He is and He also tells us who we are and what He has done for us and what He will do for us. He expresses His vows to us through His Word. And our vow is a one liner: I believe. That's it. But this one liner is not the end of it, because faith (believing) produces a fruit, and that fruit is obedience, and thats why faith without works is dead. So in this covenant relationship, God says I love you in a trillion different ways and you say I love You in a single way, by believing in Him, and this faith is ultimately expressed through its fruit, which is obedience.

This may sound farfetched, but it's true and it can be your reality if you have surrendered your life to Christ. The ability to obey is made possible by the finished work of Jesus at the cross. He first loved us and chose us, thus making it possible for us to love Him and express this love through faith and its fruit, obedience. Without Him loving us, there is no us loving Him. In different parts of this book I will be mentioning obedience and I want you to keep in mind that obedience is God's love language and thus obeying God is expressing our love for God, obeying God is choosing to love God in the way He wants to be loved. Also remember that obedience is a fruit of faith, much like patience is a fruit of the Spirit. You can't have patience apart from the Spirit, in the same way you can't have obedience apart from faith. If you struggle to obey, its because you struggle to believe.

DEATH TO DOUBT

Think of yourself as a grip holding on to the all knowing, all sovereign, all good and able God. The power to tighten the grip is called faith. The power to loosen the grip is called doubt. How tight or how loose the grip is depends on these two choices, what would you choose?

The choice seems rather simple to any sane person: faith. When we choose faith, we are choosing to tighten our grip on God. Jesus referred to this as abiding in Him. This is not task oriented but relationship oriented. We don't hold onto Him and tighten our grip on Him when we want something from Him. We ask Him for things because we have our grip on Him. We ask from relationship not outside of relationship. When the asking comes from a place of relationship, we will wait patiently but when the asking comes from outside the relationship, then it's easy to lose heart. Remember faith is a covenant, a covenant God never breaks. This is our security. Letting go of faith is letting go of our assurance.

Doubt is to lack confidence in God and His Word; it's to consider His judgment unlikely. It's saying God, "I don't really think you can do that. I'm not sure that's in your alley." It's this lack of confidence in God's Word that led to the fall of humanity at the Garden of Eden. Now, I am not saying doubt is the same thing as disobedience. You can have doubts and still choose to trust and obey God. It's rare, but it's possible. What I am saying is, doubt can quickly escalate you to unbelief and disobedience.

You've heard it said that the grass is always greener on the other side. The truth is the grass is always greener on where Jesus dwells, in you. Most times when you are in the process, you begin to envy the people who seem to have what you are waiting for. You begin to think that life will be much better when you are where they are. You begin to think that life will be better when your dreams come true, when you are living your calling. When you have your dream job. When your book is published. When you graduate. When your company takes off. When you minister to thousands. When you accomplish your goals and when you exercise the fullness of your potential. I'm not saying there is anything wrong or bad about this, but none of these things make your life better. What makes life the best it can be is to be in the presence of God. A place where we have full confidence in God, no matter what stage or season of life we are in, this is the best life.

Ask yourself. Are you living your life by fully believing that God is Who He says He is and He will do exactly what He says He will do? Are you committed in this covenant relationship? Are you living your life by taking God at His Word? Are you asking God for what you're asking God for in confidence that He will do it?

When you read the four gospels, you find many instances where Jesus is rebuking doubt or unbelief, probably more than He rebuked anything else.

Aside from rebuking pharisees. One time His disciples prayed for a child who was demon possessed and the demon wasn't bothered at all. The boy's dad then brings the child to Jesus and asked Him to heal the boy because the disciples had failed. At this point Jesus is not amused by the doubting hearts of the disciples and says, "You faithless and corrupt people! How long must I be with you and put up with you?" (Mathew 17:17, NLT) This is just one story of Jesus rebuking unbelief and doubt. When you take your time to read through the gospels, you can't escape the question; why did Jesus have such emphasis against doubt?

The Word says "without faith it's impossible to please God" which only means "It's impossible to please God when we live in doubt". This might be hard to accept because doubt has become second nature to a lot of Christians today. The Church has become weak because the body has allowed doubt to creep in. I'm tempted to think that we have become ignorant. Maybe we've lost touch with Kingdom reality. Maybe there is something that the early church knew that we don't, maybe there is something that God reveals to a few and the rest of us are just in the dark. And if you're not in this elite group of people that receive these revelations then you've missed it, sorry. But this train of thought is absolutely false; because when you read the Bible you realize that in this mayhem and confusion, the Bible offers clarity to everyone.

The one thing doubt can't co-exist with is faith. This means faith is the only thing that can eliminate doubt in our lives. But this is not new information to you, is it? Chances are you already know this. You also know that "faith comes by hearing, and hearing by the Word of God." (Romans 10:17). Which means without consistent devotion on the Word of God, our faith won't be built and if our faith won't be built, doubt will remain in our hearts. There are no shortcuts to get rid of doubt; we have to be full of the Word of God, which builds our faith, which eliminates doubt. But we already know this, yet we somehow don't take this part of building our faith too seriously.

I hope what I say next will challenge you to take this seriously. In Ephesians 6 Paul talks about how we don't fight against flesh and blood but against evil rulers and authorities of the unseen world, against mighty powers in this dark world, and against evil spirits in the heavenly places. He then goes on to describe what is called the Armor of God and he instructs believers to put this on so we are equipped to resist the devil. Now, before I go any further, Paul says resist, not defeat, because the enemy is already defeated, all we do is resist the lies and the enemy will flee (James 4:7, NIV). Paul then goes on to describe individual pieces to carry. I will only focus on one, the shield of faith, which has the power to stop the fiery arrows of the devil. Now here's what I want you to imagine. Imagine yourself carrying this shield of faith, and then somehow doubt creeps into your heart, and we know doubt and faith can't co-exist, what's going to happen? You were tightening the grip and suddenly you're loosening the grip. What's going to happen?

If taking God at His Word is a shield, then doubting is a suicide mission. Faith is the weapon ordained by God to stop the fiery (burning strongly) arrows of the enemy. The confidence we have in God and His Word is what protects us from the enemies attacks. Doubting is giving up this shield, thus being vulnerable in front of the enemy who brings a nuclear bomb to a knife fight, allowing his fiery arrows to come right through us.

It is through doubt that the enemy has managed to accomplish so much damage and death. Doubt can kill your dreams. Doubt can kill your calling. Doubt can kill your marriage. Doubt can kill your relationships. Doubt can kill your progress. Doubt can kill your miracle. Doubt can kill your breakthrough. Doubt can even lead to eternal death. Doubt can accomplish so much damage in your life.

Peter is known for his five seconds walking on water fame. The second he started doubting he started sinking. He had loosened his grip on God. Most of us can attest to this. Most of us are living in doubt in this moment.

The danger we are in because of the friendship we have developed with doubt is deadly. Majority of us have grown to accept doubt while we are in the process. When God seems to take longer than what we had anticipated, we begin to have doubt. Instead of using the process as the opportunity to please and worship God, we use it as an opportunity to display our lack of confidence in God. This is the tragedy we display to God when we allow doubt into our hearts.

This could be a life changing truth if we take it seriously, if we believe it, if we apply it. God is good and never changing. The rules of battle will not change, the shield will remain to be faith, and the killer will remain to be the devil through his top ammo, doubt.

03

{ACT 1}
THE IN BETWEEN

The right view of the process

We have established that no one is exempted from the process; we all go through the process. This makes having the right view of the process monumental to your life. How you view the process will determine how much you progress in this life. What you think of the process will determine the course of your life. It will determine the amount of miracles you see. It will determine whether or not you witness the "immeasurably more than what you ask or imagine" in your lifetime.

Put yourself in the shoes of Noah. God speaks to you about building an ark and telling people that they should repent, He is about to wipe out everything (Genesis 5-9). You take Him at His Word and start the building project, and year after year nothing happens, ten years pass, nothing happens, twenty years pass, nothing happens, fifty years pass, nothing happens, one hundred years pass and nothing happens. Imagine how the people must have thought Noah was a joke when year after year the flood wasn't showing up? People must've thought he was crazy, but one hundred and twenty years went and boom, the manifestation was there. Noah must've known something about the process; otherwise he would've thrown in the towel already in the thirtieth year. You need to develop the right view of the process; otherwise you will quit when the process grows harder.

We have established that we walk by faith and not by sight. This way of living is the one that pleases God. Living our lives by taking Him at His Word not by the merit of what we can see. This truth reveals faith as the only opportunity we have to please God. Ultimately this truth makes the process a wonderful opportunity to please (worship) God because faith is magnified in the process.

This revelation has personally changed my view of the process. Knowing that holding on to God's promise is a display of my trust in Him has revolutionized my view of the process. I now no longer look at the process as God delaying His answers to me, or God not carrying my request with as much weight as I do. I now look at the process as a wonderful opportunity to please God by believing that He will in fact do exactly what He says He will do. I now look at the process as that rare opportunity to demonstrate how much I trust in my God. Because I know that God is not interested in me believing Him on the merit of what I can see, but believing Him on the basis of what I cannot see. Every time I find myself in the process is every time I am blessed with the opportunity to express how much I love my God. Faith is His love language. Remember?

The process is an opportunity to display how much you trust your God, how you know that without a doubt He is faithful, and no matter how long it takes, He will answer. He will deliver His end of the vows, for His glory.

Faith is fully displayed and magnified when we are in the waiting period. Faith is given a spot light when we are waiting on God; which means its in-the-process moments and times that we please God the most because these are the times our trust in God is given the spotlight. So I want to challenge you to change your view of the process, start viewing the process as the opportunity to please God, the opportunity to express how much you love God by trusting Him.

Now, this is not about performance or works. This view of the process is because we know and believe Jesus finished everything at the cross, we know and believe that Jesus is doing a perfect job as our Great High Priest before God. He is interceding for us. This view of the process is because we know that God loves us so much, that He didn't withhold anything, not even His Son, Jesus Christ, from us, so why would He withhold anything He has promised us? This view of the process is purely based on how good God is, how gracious He is and how faithful He is. We know that God never changes, that He is ever faithful and that when we go to Him and pray He is a good Father and He answers, this is the absolute truth. So no matter how long it takes, or how much worse the circumstances get, He is good and faithful and He will answer. It's in this belief that this view of the process is derived from. Every time you find yourself waiting on God for something, you are graced with a stage, with God in the audience; is God having a great time watching you? Again, this is not works. Faith is a covenant. You are already His. He is already yours. No performance. No works. But we should delight in His joy and pleasure. You are graced with a stage; God is your only audience. Is He having a good time?

NOT THE SIZE BUT THE OBJECT OF FAITH

In Luke chapter 17 Jesus was talking about offense and forgiveness with His disciples, and when He told them "even when a person offends you seven times in a day and comes back asking for forgiveness, forgive them," the disciples replied "Increase our faith". But what's interesting is what Jesus says next, "If you have faith as a mustard seed, you can say to this mulberry tree, 'Be pulled up by the roots and be planted in the sea,' and it would obey you." (Luke 17:6). Now it doesn't take a genius to notice the massive difference between these two objects: the faith is extremely small but the result is extremely colossal.

The monumental thing is not the size of faith; it's the object of faith. You can have moon-sized faith in yourself and it won't produce any power; it won't even move sand castles. Only when God is the object of our faith are we able to witness immeasurably more than what we can imagine or ask.

This is a self-based generation. It's all about me, myself and I. Believing in self is a very popular message these days, it's what motivational speakers and some pastors preach. We've grown to place a lot of faith in self. Self has become the object of faith for a lot of us. We primarily believe in who we are and what we can do. God is simply a means for the cause of self.

To believe in something we must first know that object. The issue with this generation is that we know so little of God. So we settle for the object we know the most, self. Who is the object of your faith? The right response is God, but before you say this, take time and introspect. Is God really the object of your faith?

FAITH IS NURTURED NOT MICROWAVED

We just saw that it's not about the size of faith but the object of faith. The object of faith is the one producing the results, not the size. The Triune God is the object of our Faith. Jesus is the object of our faith. Now Jesus used the Words "Ye of little faith" many a time. This doesn't contradict the truth that it's not about the size but the object.

In Mathew 17:20, the words little faith is the Greek Word *oligopistian* which originates from two words: *oligos* which means small, brief, small; hence of time, little while, short time. The second word is *pistis*, which comes from the word peithó which means persuade, be persuaded, come to trust. Pistis for the believer is "God's divine persuasion". It is God's warranty that guarantees the fulfillment of His Word. Putting this together, we come to a revelation that you of little faith means; "You who respond only for a while, only for a short time, only briefly to God's divine persuasion" and we see this true when Peter responded to God's divine persuasion when he started walking on water but after a short while, he doubted and started sinking and what did Jesus say? "Ye of little faith" or simply put "You who respond only for a while, only for a short time, only briefly to God's divine persuasion"

In this time of being in the process, God is divinely persuading you into your calling, into your audacious dream, into your breakthrough. You have to respond fully, you have to fully believe in Him and His Word. Faith is not a brief response. Faith is a full response.

MUSTARD SEED BELIEVERS

Jesus used the mustard seed to illustrate faith many times. "He said to them, "Because of your little faith. For truly, I say to you, if you have faith like a grain of mustard seed, you will say to this mountain, 'Move from here to there,' and it will move, and nothing will be impossible for you."" (Matthew 17:20, ESV). In another place Jesus says, "The kingdom of heaven is like a mustard seed, which a man took and sowed in his field, ³²*which indeed is the least of all the seeds; but when it is grown it is greater than the herbs and becomes a tree* , so that the birds of the air come and nest in its branches." (Matthew 13:31-32).

To fully understand why Jesus specifically chose the mustard seed in many occasions to illustrate faith, we have to understand the mustard seed and herb. Jesus lived in Israel, which is found on the Mediterranean. Mustard that comes from that region is the Black Mustard. It is believed that Jesus was talking about this type of mustard in His illustration.

I studied the nature of this plant. Black Mustard is known to be an invasive plant that will consume the entire field in a short time. One of its unique features is that it grows so tightly together and forms an unsurpassable thicket that becomes a home for other species including birds. Faith like a mustard seed is not little faith. It is a consuming faith. It is faith that will consume your whole life. It's not a moment-by-moment, situation-by-situation faith; it is an all-in kind of faith. Jesus was saying that if you have faith like a child where you take God at His Word, nothing would be impossible to you. Child-like faith testifies of the sovereignty of the object of your faith and not the size of your faith. Child-like faith glorifies God because it says my circumstances will not determine my outcome. Just like how small a mustard seed is, but when planted it invades and consumes the entire farm. A mustard believer is a person who lives their life by fully believing that God is who He says He is and He will do exactly what He says He will do.

THE SOIL THAT UNLEASHES THE MUSTARD SEED

Faith begins with God divinely pursuing us. Our response is what determines our faith. Do we fully respond or do we briefly respond? We are the ones to make this choice. God's major tool for His divine persuasion of us is His Word. That's why the Bible says, "Faith comes by hearing and hearing by the Word of God" (Romans 10:17).

For the all-consuming nature and potential of the mustard seed to come to life, it must be planted. This makes the soil the most important aspect in unleashing the potential of the child-like faith. Without the soil, the seed doesn't come to life. God is divinely persuading us, throwing into our hearts the mustard seeds but the condition of the soil is what will unleash the potential of the seed.

The soil is your heart. What's the condition of your heart? Is your heart set in a condition that will unleash the power of this child-like faith?

A mustard seed is planted, not microwaved. Faith is not microwaved, it is planted and nurtured. For what is planted to bring forth fruit, nurturing must take place. There are no shortcuts to growing your faith. That's the problem with a lot of us, we try and microwave faith and that's why it's short lived, it's brief, it's only for a while, we of little faith. Jesus used an agricultural term for a reason. For a child-like faith to unleash its potential and power, we must make sure the condition of our hearts is fertile and nurturing.

It's exactly what the parable of the sower talks about. And as he sowed, some seed fell on the rocks, some on the wayside, some by the thorns and some by the good soil. The integrity and potential of the seed was the same, but it was unleashed on different scales based on the nature of the soil. In hard ground it produced nothing, in thorny ground it joined the "ye of little faith club" and the seed that fell on the good soil produced fruit. Even the good soil has degrees of fruitfulness. Not all of them unleashed the fullest potential of the seed, as the Bible says, "But he who received seed on the good ground is he who hears the Word and understands it, who indeed bears fruit and produces: some a hundredfold, some sixty, some thirty" (Matthew 13:23).

FEARLESS OBEDIENCE

This nurturing is called fearless obedience. Fearless obedience is the ingredient that nurtures your faith, which strengthens your faith and helps your faith grow. Before I explain this, let me make one thing clear, saying fearless obedience implies that there is fearful obedience. And you are right, there is obedience that stems from fear, you obey because you fear the consequences, much like how most kids obey school regulations. But I am talking about fearless obedience, obedience that stems from love. You obey because you love God, not because you are afraid of Him.

Fearless obedience is what purifies the conditions of our hearts making it possible for faith to grow and produce more fruit. A fearlessly obedient heart is what unleashes the fullest potential of a child-like faith. It's the heart that takes God at His Word even when things don't make sense. A fearlessly obedient heart is the heart that fully responds and commits to God's divine persuasion. Is your heart fearlessly obedient to God and His Word?

Like I said before, faith comes first, then obedience follows because obedience is a fruit of faith. So I am not in conflict with what I've said before here. If faith produces no obedience then your faith will never grow, and it'll eventually die. The more obedience your faith produces, the stronger your faith will grow thus unleashing its fullest potential.

Let me put it in another way. Faith comes by hearing and hearing by the Word of God. This is proof that faith comes first. Faith then produces a fruit called obedience. This means we are only able to love God when we first believe. When this faith produces our love for God, and this love is expressed through obedience, then our faith is made stronger. What grows our faith from weak to stronger is our love for God. This love is directly tied to our obedience. This is why Christ is the only One who completely loves God, because He is the only One who completely obeys God without failing.

Faith and obedience form a circle of life. Obedience is not possible without faith. Faith will eventually die without obedience. So when I say a fearlessly obedient heart unleashes the fullest potential of childlike faith, I mean, for your faith to be fully unleashed, this faith and obedience's circle of life has to be in motion.

Again, it's not about the size of faith; it's about the object of faith. The object of faith is God. Faith starts with God divinely persuading us. He pursues us because He gave us freewill. He wants us to choose to be in relationship with Him and to follow where He leads us. How we respond to this pursuit is what determines our faith. But the condition of our hearts must be nurtured with fearless obedience to unleash the full potential of the childlike mustard seed faith. In the process God is divinely persuading you to remain faithful in your faith covenant while waiting on Him. In fact God is persuading you right now while reading this book. What's it going to be? Are you going to respond to His divine persuasion and wait on Him faithfully? Are you going to fully respond to Him even when what you're waiting for is not manifested? Are you going to set this cirlce of life of faith and obedience in motion? What's it going to be?

04

The process affords us ultimate worship

"What happens when we worship? We remember, we return and we reconnect." - Steffany Gretzinger

When we praise God we say things like "God you are good! Jesus you overcame the grave! How great is our God! No other Name like the Name of Jesus! and many amazing things about the character of all three Persons of God: The Father, Jesus and The Holy Spirit.

For most of us, worship is the Sunday morning experience where great music is played and amazing worship leaders lead us into worship. A lot of us have associated worship with music and declarations of the majesty of God.

There's another dimension to worship: "Worship is a lifestyle. Worship is not a part of your life. Worship is your life. Every activity can be transformed into an act of worship, when you do it for the praise and the glory and the pleasure of God" (Rick Warren, 68).

Worship is not just music, but worship is our life. We can turn anything we do into worship. Whether it is work or eating or chores, as long as we do it as if we are doing it for the glory of God, It is a form of worship.

Worship is a big deal to God. God desires worship. In fact Jesus said: "A time will come, however, indeed it is already here, when true (genuine) worshippers will worship the Father in spirit and in truth (reality); for the Father is seeking just such people as these as His worshipers" (John 4:23, AMPC).

In this scripture, the word worshippers comes from the Greek word proskuneó which comes from words *pros* which means towards and *kyeo* which means to kiss- to kiss the ground when prostrating before a superior. It's the readiness to fall down/prostrate oneself to adore on one's knees. In the passage we just read, Jesus says the Father is seeking people who will worship Him in spirit and in truth (reality). God is seeking people who will fall down and prostrate themselves before Him in adoration, both in the spirit but also in truth (reality); this act of worship must have outward reality.

R. Kent Hughes said, "God desires worship above all else. Thus, every man *(or woman)* who calls himself a Christian must understand that worship is the ultimate priority of his/*her* life (111).

God desires worship. God loves worship. When we engage in worship, we are ministering to God. We are giving Him pleasure and joy.

I want to acknowledge that there's more to worship than just music and declarations, more than just transforming every activity into an act of worship. There's the ultimate worship. It's called faith. Like we saw previously, that faith is living our lives by fully believing that God is who He says He is, and will do exactly what He says He will do.

Simply put, faith is taking God at His Word. Which means when God says He is good, you believe that He is good. When He says, "I am the good shepherd" (John 10:11, NIV), you believe Him. When He says, "Fear not, for I am with you" (Isaiah 41:10), you believe Him. When He says, "Take delight in the Lord, and He shall give you the desires of your heart," (Psalm 37:4, NIV), you believe Him. When He says, "be merciful just as your Father is merciful" (Luke 6:36, NIV), you take Him at His Word and obey what He says. When He says, "love your neighbor as yourself" (Matthew 19:19, NIV), you take Him at His Word and spread this love. When He says, "If you believe, you will receive whatever you ask for in prayer," (Matthew 21:22, NIV), you take Him at His Word. And this list can go on and on.

What I love about worship and praise is that we declare God's greatness, we sing of His goodness, we shout of His praises and we acknowledge His majesty. It's exactly what Steffany said, "We remember, we return and we reconnect". We remember how great He is, we return to His presence and we reconnect with him. Worship is simply remembering, returning and re-connecting.

But what I love most about faith is that; faith is living out the praise and worship. It all hangs in our faith. The depth of our praise and worship hangs in our faith. I'm not just talking about us believing what we sing about but I am talking about us living what we sing about.

God is not interested in us just shouting He is good. He is interested in us believing He is good. He is interested in us believing He is faithful. Believing that He will renew our strength. Believing that He will make us prosperous. Believing that He has prepared greater things for us in the life to come for His glory, and it's this faith that gives new life to our proclamations of His goodness. God is ultimately interested in us believing Him.

The waiting period is a wonderful opportunity to minister to God by taking Him at His Word. What is God saying to you in this season of your life?

Is He telling you to be still? Give Him pleasure by being still.

Is He telling to wait patiently? Give Him pleasure by being patient.

Is He telling you to hold on? Give Him pleasure by holding on.

Is He telling you to take a step of faith? Give Him pleasure by taking a step of faith.

The process is a wonderful opportunity to minister to God. To give Him pleasure. To give Him joy by holding-on to faith. Clinging to the covenant. God delights in faith more than anything else.

Faith unlocks the depth of worship and praise in every minute and every hour of our lives.

Faith is saying, God You are faithful, and then remaining steadfast in your calling in the midst of pain, setbacks and discouragement. Worship doesn't any get any better than this.

Faith is saying, God You are able and then you chase after your dream when your circumstances say it's impossible, when every door seem to be closing. Worship doesn't any get any better than this.

Faith is saying, God You will bless me in your perfect time, I won't take things in my own hands nor will I complain. Worship doesn't get any better than this.

Faith is worship. Faith is the only place where we live out our worship every second and every hour of everyday. Live a life of praise and worship by fully believing that God is who He says He is, and will do exactly what He says He will do.

In the four gospels, Jesus talks a lot about the Kingdom culture, and His emphasis was mostly based on the inner character. He spoke about love, forgiveness, grace, mercy and kindness. In John 15:7, He instructs us that all He has taught us needs to take root inside of our being. Obedience is a display of faith. You can't obey when you don't believe. Disobedience and faith can't co-exist. In this context, every time we encounter a situation where Jesus has given us a command, it is a time we are graced with a stage to worship God by obeying His Word. I'm talking about worshipping God with our responses, reactions and attitude all the time and especially when we are in the process.

When someone treats you unfairly, but you extend grace towards him or her and treat him or her better than they deserve to be treated, you have engaged in worship because you've taken God at His Word when He said, "Be merciful for I am merciful."

When what you thought was the opportunity to progress from where you are to where you are called, is out the window and no longer an option available for you, but you still choose to smile and say, "God You are good and faithful, You will open another door for me", you have engaged in worship. Because you've taken God at His Word when He said, "For My thoughts are not your thoughts, Nor are your ways My ways," says the LORD. "For as the heavens are higher than the earth, So are My ways higher than your ways, And My thoughts than your thoughts." (Isaiah 55:8-9).

I don't know if you're catching this. Don't segment praise and worship in your life. Praise and worship is your life. Every minute, every hour, it's all faith. Take Him at His Word. Not by His manifestation, but at His Word.

In every circumstance you face while you are in the process, you are presented with an opportunity to worship and minister to God by believing in what He says about that situation. When you respond with faith, you are engaging in the ultimate worship to God. This is the right view of the process. How many opportunities of deeper worship have you wasted by giving up? Compromising? Taking matters into your own hands? It's not too late. You are in the process right now, waiting on God for something; it could be your dream, God's call on your life, a miracle, or a breakthrough. You have a grand opportunity to worship God. What are you going to do with this opportunity? Are you going to break the pattern? Are you going to minister to God? Are you going to meet His deepest desire? Are you going to give Him pleasure?

The process is your pulpit

You're the worship leader

You worship with your faith

The stronger the faith

The pure the worship

Embrace the process

Unleash the worship

It's a privilege

Let me clear something here, so that you don't misunderstand me. This is not about works. The central focus of everything here is God. The fact that we are even able to delight in pleasing God is an act of grace. All this is possible because of what Christ did at the cross. Every bit of this echoes grace. Our act of pleasing God is not an act of returning a favor or a transaction. It's all possible because of His grace, so no one can boast and say I please God more than the next person. His abundant grace enables us to please Him. It's all about Him.

FAITH IS THE SWEETEST AROMA TO GOD

Our praise and worship is offered to God as a sweet aroma. This started in the Old Testament during which priests offered incense offering to God (Read Leviticus 2:2), and God would receive it as a sweet smelling aroma. But this was a foreshadow of what we, as new covenant children of God, will offer God. The great thing is that we don't have to burn anything, but we now offer the sacrifices of praise with our lips (Hebrews 12:15). Praise is a form of worship. But this sacrifice of praise isn't confined within the lips. Because what's stronger than what you proclaim is the faith behind what you proclaim. The strength of the aroma you offer God lies in your faith.

Every time we worship the Lord, what He receives is a sweet aroma, and that's why worship is ministering to God. When we engage in an activity as a form of worship, we basically offer the Lord a sweet smelling aroma. It pleases Him; it gives Him pleasure, that's why God loves worship.

Faith is the highest form of worship. Faith is the sweetest smelling aroma to God. When we respond in faith, we offer the Lord the sweetest smelling aroma. We give Him pleasure and joy.

In the process is the time when our faith is most active. The process is the time when our ministry to the Lord is the sweetest. When we respond with faith, His alter is filled with the sweetest smelling aroma, it gives Him joy and pleasure.

This is the right view of the process

It's not time wasted

It's a one-of-a-kind opportunity

The kind that gives God pleasure

Take Him at His Word

Press on

Don't give up on your God given dream

Don't abandon God's call on your life

Believe in what you're praying for

This is your ministry to the Lord

This is the highest form of worship

Break out and dance

He has not forgotten your prayer

He has simply blessed you with an opportunity

A divine opportunity for worship

Worship at the highest level

Embrace it. Enjoy it. Own it.

blessed to last *blessed to last* **blessed to last** *blessed to last* **blessed to last** *blessed to last-* **blessed to last** *blessed to last* **blessed to last** *blessed to last* **bless- ed to last** *blessed to last* **blessed to last** *blessed to last-* **blessed to last** *blessed to last* **blessed to last** *blessed to last* **blessed to last** *blessed to last* **blessed to last** *blessed to last* **blessed to last** *blessed to last* **blessed to last** *blessed to last* **blessed to last** *blessed to last* **blessed to last** *b*

God is building you up for impact

05

Dust off
the painting

This is the era of purpose and destiny. This is the age of dreamers and go-get-ters. Living in this current time and not having a dream is considered a life without significance. Dreams fuel our will to wake up every morning and give our very best into making them come true. So dreaming big is the least of our problems. Our problem is that we either stop short or jeopardize our destinies. Our issue is that we don't know how to wait on God. Most of us live our lives short of what we dreamt of and what we were called to do be-cause we stopped short. Dreams are on full supply, waiting on God is what's out of stock. Being unfaithful in the process is what's killing our dreams and callings more than anything else. The process is inevitable, but most of us aren't prepared to go through it. So when we find ourselves going through it, we give up. We feel cheated because nobody told us it was going to be like this. We don't see why we have to go through it. I mean, God is able, so why not skip it? This act will deal with the simple reality that God is interested in your long-term impact, not just results. For there to be long-term impact,

God must build up your character and prepare you. This preparation happens in the process.

KEEP THE MAIN THING THE MAIN THING

Every God given dream we conceive. Every calling we have upon our lives. Every assignment we are given on this earth by God lies in this scripture as its foundation: "Then God blessed them, and God said to them, "Be fruitful and multiply; fill the earth and *subdue it*; *have dominion* over the fish of the sea, over the birds of the air, and over every living thing that moves on the earth" (Genesis 1:28, KJV).

The human race was conceived out of love. He loved us before He formed us. He created us for fellowship with Him. Our reason for existence is to have fellowship with God. It was not out of assignment we were created, but for fellowship. The one thing Heaven and Earth have in common for the life of the believer is the worship and the pursuit of God. Wherever God decides to plant the human race, the one thing that will remain is the worship and the pursuit of God. This is why we exist, for fellowship. The pursuit of God is always the primary thing.

But the Lord is a God of purpose. He created us for fellowship but He planted us on earth for a purpose. We exist to fellowship with the living God. But we exist on this planet earth for a specific purpose. This purpose is what we just saw in Genesis 1:28, to subdue and have dominion here on earth. Establishing His righteous rule. Imparting heaven on earth. To subdue means to bring under control. We were created for fellowship, but we were planted here on earth to establish His Kingdom "On earth as it is in Heaven" (Matthew 6:10).

...........................WALKED WITH GOD

A good example is what we know of Enoch. The Word says, "Enoch walked with God." Walking with establishes two things: First, that He was always in fellowship with God; and second, is that he was always on God's mission. He existed for fellowship but He was on earth for a mission. We later learn in Hebrews that Enoch pleased God. Enoch pleased God because He exercised both ends of His existence.

Most of us Christians hang on one end of this spectrum. We either fellowship with God or we are busy pursuing purpose and calling. But a life that's pleasing to God is a life of the balance He created. Fellowship first. Assignment second. These two are simultaneous but fellowship is the ever constant. The assignment can change; a good example is our life in Heaven. No human really knows what we will be doing there; whatever it is it will be secondary to the primary thing, which is fellowship. We find life and fulfillment in fellowship with God-this is why we exist. We find impact and purpose in assignment-this is why we are on earth.

...........................WALKED WITH MEN

Today people stand a very good chance of walking with men. We have elevated the opinion of men over what we should be and do and we have forsaken what God has called us to do. We have become ineffective citizens of Heaven. We fellowship with God but we receive our assignment from men. That's why we have ceased to shape culture, because we've allowed the culture to shape our callings. We have diminished what Jesus restored at the cross. Jesus restored men's fellowship with God, eternally. He also restored man's dominion and the subduing assignment he was given by God. We have deprived the Holy Spirit the chance to teach us all things. We have quenched the Spirit of God.

So where does the process fit into this family made of fellowship and purpose, you might ask. Jesus Himself paints a complete picture of this family for us in the New Testament. He said, "Follow Me, and I will make you become fishers of men" (Mark 1:17, ESV). The first thing is following the Lord, pursuing God, fellowship with Him. Then there's becoming which is the process. And there is the purpose (fishers of men). This is the picture He painted for us. Highlighting that every assignment has a process.

WE CANNOT REPAINT THE PICTURE

After God had created Adam and Eve, He gave them the whole world. He literary gave them the whole world. He told them to "Be fruitful and multiply; fill the earth and subdue it; have dominion over the fish of the sea, over the birds of the air, and over every living thing that moves on the earth." (Genesis 1:28). This was God's original design. God entrusted the whole world to Adam and Eve because they were in perfect relationship with God. They were fully set apart for God's purpose. God could entrust the whole earth to them because they were in complete obedience to Him, they were fully surrendered to God. It was in this communion, abiding, obedience and surrender, God entrusted them with the whole world. He knew they will rule the earth with righteousness. They will impart the Kingdom of Heaven on earth. They will glorify God with all that they are and do.

But of course this didn't last. The enemy deceived Eve. And when she doubted the boundary God had set for them, she disobeyed God and declared independence from God. That was the fall of man, as we know it. Sin and death entered the world. Every human born after that was born a sinner, with the exception of Jesus.

Every child is born a sinner. Every baby is born flawed, with broken character. Born with pride, full of deceit. Born an enemy of God. God's original design was broken. Man is no longer in perfect obedience to God. He is now sinful in his nature. His dominion over the earth is broken and his rule is no longer righteous. In his current state he can longer be trusted to carry the task originally assigned to him by his Creator. Tragic, right? But this is not the end of the story, because God is love and He loves us. Right after Adam and Eve's sin, He began the work to redeem us. So the assignment to have dominion and subdue the earth didn't die with Adam and his wife. They might've handed their right to rule over earth to Satan when they fell into sin. Which gave Satan the authority to subdued the earth with sin and darkness. But throughout this time the hope of mankind lay in the promise of a Messiah who would take up the keys to rule and have dominion over earth as how it was originally. This promise was given to Eve in Genesis 3:15.

Thousands of years later God fulfills this promise through the birth, death and resurrection of His beloved Son, Jesus Christ. Jesus comes, restores and takes back what Adam lost. Through Adam death came into the world, through Jesus everlasting life became a gift available for all who believe (See Romans 5:17-21). Through Adam, humankind was subdued by the world but through Christ and the power of His Holy Spirit inside us, we once again get to have dominion and are equipped to subdue the world. But this is made possible through the work of sanctification done by His Holy Spirit who lives inside us. This happens through the renewal of the mind (Romans 12:2) that results in transformation and conformity to the image of Jesus Christ. (We'll get more into this in the next act).

Why am I bringing this up? Because to experience the fullness of this take back era, the restoration era, we must be in a continual state of realizing and coming to terms with our spiritual bankruptcy. As born again Christians, we are in a continual state of transformation. Every manifestation is dependent upon the process of sanctification.

By His grace He freely transforms us

On His terms and time He manifests

Dreams and prayers for His glory

06

Modeled for us and commissioned to us

Our Lord and Savior Jesus Christ rescued us from God's wrath and eternal judgment. He paid the price of sin and death for all mankind to restore two things. First, to restore the fellowship between you and God, and through the work of Jesus, you now can have eternal fellowship with God. Second, to restore your authority to subdue the earth. You can see this more clearly in Matthew 28:18-20.

> And Jesus came and spoke to them, saying, "All authority has been given to Me in heaven and on earth. Go therefore and make disciples of all the nations, baptizing them in the name of the Father and of the Son and of the Holy Spirit, teaching them to observe all things that I have commanded you; and lo, I am with you always, even to the end of the age." Amen.

This is the fulfilled purpose of God for planting us here on earth. Note that when God gave Adam and Eve their purpose on this earth, they were already disciples of God. Putting the scripture in Genesis 1:28 and Mathew 28:18-20 together we find a fulfilled purpose for our lives here on earth.

"All authority has been given to Me in heaven and on earth. Go therefore and make disciples of all the nations, baptizing them in the name of the Father and of the Son and of the Holy Spirit, teaching them to observe all things that I have commanded you; and lo, I am with you always, *even* to the end of the age." And "Be fruitful and multiply; fill the earth and *subdue it; have dominion* over the fish of the sea, over the birds of the air, and over every living thing that moves on the earth"

In this new covenant of Grace, not only are we called to be disciples who fellowship with their Lord, but we are called to make disciples of all nations. Teaching them the way of life Jesus modeled for us so as to subdue this earth and exercise our dominion over all creation and establish His righteous rule until He comes back for His Church.

When Jesus lived on earth, He shaped and impacted culture more than anyone else in human history. He subdued the earth more than anyone, ever. He imparted the culture of His Kingdom here on earth. Jesus was a status quo disrupter and a culture shaper. He did this by holding firm and exalting the Word of God. Jesus said: "For I have not spoken on My own authority; but the Father who sent Me gave Me a command, what I should say and what I should speak." (John 12:49). Jesus is our model for shaping culture. The call to shape culture is a call for every Christian. Regardless of who you are and where you are in life. This is our reason for being here on earth.

The culture of heaven is seen through the Words of Jesus. The will of the Father is seen through the actions of Jesus. His Words and actions were synonymous. When Jesus was teaching His disciples to pray, to what we commonly know today as the Lord's Prayer, the lines read "...Your Kingdom come, your will be done, on earth as it is in Heaven..." (Matthew 6:10, NIV). Bringing the Kingdom of Heaven on earth and His will being done here on earth as it is being done in Heaven constitute as a strong call to shape culture. Jesus modeled best this powerful prayer. All that He said and did was according to the Father, who is in Heaven, who is in fact Heaven.

God is not interested in results. God is interested in impact. Culture is not shaped by results; it's shaped by impact, and impact requires character. God is using the process to build your character so you can glorify Him when what you are believing Him for is manifested.

So while you are ministering to Him,

Transformation is happening within,

To build you for impact,

For His glory.

THE CHURCH THAT SUBDUES

I don't think there's ever been a church more powerful than the first church. We read about this church in the book of Acts. This was the church that I'd like to call, the church that subdues the world. It suffered the most yet it had the most impact.

The first church was birthed in the midst of persecution. Those who professed Christ as The Lord were persecuted. At the time, Jewish leaders opposed anyone who believed that Christ is the Lord. The Romans were killing and imprisoning Christians. A good example of what happened in the times of the first church was what happened in the year 64 AD. Nero blamed Christians for the great fire that destroyed 10 of the 14 City Wards of Rome, a fire that apparently Nero himself ordered. The Historian Tacitus, not a Christian, said that Nero had the believers "torn by dogs and perished, or were nailed to crosses, or were doomed to the flames and burnt, to serve as a nightly illumination, when daylight had expired" (44). Most of the Christians at that time were butchered, but they remained faithful to the cause of Christ. They were deeply convicted about Christ and the mission He assigned them here on earth. And they were prepared for it. The founders of the first church were the apostles of Jesus; they had been in the process from the time Jesus had called them to the day of Pentecost and beyond. The process was a very crucial stage for them to go through so they can live out their purpose in a way that glorifies God. Pentecost day was their first graduation. They were ready. They had become fishers of men. They thrived in the midst of opposition. They glorified God even when persecuted. And the church grew.

Another great persecution began in 303 AD, under Emperor Diocletian. The empire's second in command, Galerius, was the mastermind engineering the persecution policy, which he continued even after the death of Diocletian. For 8 years, official decrees ordered Christians out of public office, scriptures confiscated, church buildings destroyed, leaders arrested, and pagan sacrifices required. All reliable methods of torture were mercilessly employed – wild beasts, burning, stabbing, crucifixion, and the rack. But they were all to no avail. The penetration of faith across the empire was so pervasive that the church could not be intimidated nor destroyed. In 311 AD, the same Galerius, shortly before his death, weak and diseased, issued an "edict of tolerance." This included the statement that it was the duty of Christians "to pray to their God for our good estate"

The Bible as the source of life for the believer contributed heavily on western civilization. In fact it has been a major force in shaping western culture. But today the church has weakened in subduing the world. The first church was unstoppable. It prevailed through everything. It thrived in spite of the world around it. Today we are reaping what the first church sowed. Their perseverance is our inheritance.

THE X-FACTOR TO THE LIFE OF IMPACT

It is impossible to live this life of impact without the help of The Holy Spirit. The Holy Spirit is the precious and monumental gift given to us by God, to comfort us, help us and equip us to live meaningful and impactful lives. He is the X-factor. Without the Holy Spirit, praying hard for our dreams and breakthroughs would be impossible. Without the Holy Spirit, persevering when encountering opposition will be pulling nails with pliers. Without the Holy Spirit, true character development is not possible. Without the Holy Spirit, it is impossible to remain in God's Will. Without The Holy Spirit, even the Word of God becomes lifeless literature to us. When we are in the process, the Holy Spirit is our compass. We yield to His direction and conviction. Your process will not be fruitful without clinging to the Holy Spirit. Everything about the process that I talk about in this book is in direct context with the Holy Spirit being our compass when we are in the process.

Jesus said this about Him, "But the Helper (Comforter, Advocate, Intercessor—Counselor, Strengthener, Standby), the Holy Spirit, whom the Father will send in My name [in My place, to represent Me and act on My behalf], He will teach you all things. And He will help you remember everything that I have told you" (John 14:26, AMP).

This scripture comes more alive as you begin to believe God for what He has called you to do. There will be a time in your process when you need divine comfort because you're hurting. There will be a time in your process when you need divine counsel because you don't have all the answers. There will be a time in your process when you need strength because you're weak. The Holy Spirit will be there to help you through all these seasons. The process is a beautiful time of worship, delightful prayers and Christlike sanity, but there will be times of pain, confusion, stress and great uncertainty. In all these, the Holy Spirit will be by your side.

07

A character built for impact

God is a perfect God. He is perfect in every sense of the word. He knows everything, past, present and future. In fact, I like what A.W. Tozer said about God's relationship with time. He said, "Time began in Him and will end in Him. To it, He pays no tribute, and from it, He suffers no change" (16).

When God created Adam and Eve, He made them perfect. Before the fall, everything about who they are was perfect. What defined their perfection is their perfect obedience to God. This led to complete oneness with God. They were fully sanctified. God gave Adam and Eve the whole world. But none of it threatened God's position in Adam's life because God always came first. He was one with God. Everything else was secondary. Self did not drive him. Before the fall, who they were and who they were to become were the same.

But now who we are and who we ought to become are not the same. There is a huge gap in between these two realities. When Jesus died at the cross to redeem and restore God's original plan for us, He changed everything. This act of love justified us before God, which means now it's not about what we do; it's about what Jesus did at the cross. We're not accounted righteous by anything we will ever do, but by what Jesus did at the cross, and through this justification we receive the gift of eternal life. Like what the Word of God says: "for all have sinned and fall short of the glory of God, being justified freely by His grace through the redemption which is in Christ Jesus" (Romans 3:23-24).

But there's something else that comes into play here. What made Adam and Eve perfect is the simple fact that they were fully sanctified. They were fully set apart for God's purpose. But today we will only be fully set apart when we meet Christ on His second coming, either by death or His second coming. Which means, if you are living on this earth you will still fall short, you will make mistakes, you will sin, hence, the continual work of sanctification.

I am saying this as a foundation for what I am about to say next, and I want you to remember that nothing you do will earn you favor with God, we are accepted and are accounted righteous through faith by what Jesus did at the cross not what we do.

Character is highly significant in the fulfillment of your purpose. The more sanctified you are, the more equipped to subdue the world you are. The power for impact lies in sanctification. It lies in character.

I am not saying God doesn't use broken people. It will be highly hypocritical of me to think that considering I am broken and unqualified. I certainly believe that God uses broken people and unqualified people for His own glory. But regardless of how broken or how whole you are, we all go through the process. God uses the process to set us apart for His purposes so we are equipped to have impact.

God will first set apart the areas in your character that you need to be the strongest. Equipping you to withstand the temptation and attempts of the enemy to block your impact. God knows where He is calling you and what you will need to get there, remain there, have impact, shape culture and bring glory to His Name.

God has given you the dream and the calling He has given you so you can subdue your world. Subduing requires character. Character is built in the process. The Holy Spirit may be building courage and integrity in you to speak to a multitude of people because you are called to minister to thousands of people. The Holy Spirit may be building in you a spirit of discernment and confidentiality because He is calling you to counsel people. The Holy Spirit may be building your integrity because you will face many temptations where He is calling you. The only thing that will be different about you from where you are to where you are supposed to be, is your character. The more sanctified you are, the better your character becomes. This change of character only happens through the work of the Holy Spirit in us by what Jesus did at the cross. This transformation happens heavily when you allow Him to work in you during the process.

BECOMING vs. ACHIEVING

Becoming is worth much more than enormous achieving. Character is of much worth to God. Who we are inside attests to our Abba. In the four gospels, majority of the teachings of Jesus focused on the inner person. The beatitudes were all about character. His sermon on the mountain was all about character. Being the light and the salt of the earth is all about character. Becoming is inward, achieving is outward. But to maintain and protect the outward achievement, your inward becoming must be on-going. Again, it's not about achieving. It's about subduing the world, subduing its culture, its philosophy, its education, its morality, its hope, its worldview and so forth. Subduing only happens when an achievement is maintained and protected. Subduing is about consistency. Character enables us to maintain and protect what we achieve. And character is a result of becoming.

This truth is more evident through the life of king Saul. He was anointed king after the Israelites demanded Samuel to give them a king. Samuel went to God with the request. God agreed to their request. But God gave them a warning about this king they want. They didn't care. God sent Samuel to anoint Saul. Saul became the first king of Israel. The people were happy. They finally had a king.

But Saul was not prepared to be king. Saul didn't have character to be king. God told Samuel to warn the people about the king they will have. The Israelites didn't wait patiently for God's appointed time to have a king. They got what they asked for, a king. They had an achievement. He became king, but he didn't glorify God with the throne, not in the long term. He disobeyed God and caused grievance in the Heart of God. He became a maniac and consistently made chaotic decisions that led to his demise because he lacked character. He achieved without becoming, so he fell. And today we mostly talk about Saul when we talk about the cost of disobedience.

In the process of your calling and purpose being fully manifested, God is building you up so you can subdue with the influence He will give you.

In the process of being promoted, God is building you up so you can flourish for His purpose and glory where He wants to plant you.

In the process of getting a job or a new job, God is building you up so you can flourish for His purpose and glory where He wants to plant you.

In the process of preparing for marriage, God is building your character up so you can well-represent Christ's covenant keeping love with the church through your marriage.

In the process of launching your business, God is building your character up so you can glorify Him with your business for His purpose for your life.

In the process of finding your spouse, God is building your character up so you can flourish in the covenant keeping relationship for His glory. God is building your character up so you can bring out the best in your to-be spouse for God's purpose for both your lives and for His glory.

In the process of getting that next big gig, God is building you up so you can flourish for His purpose for your life in that gig and more.

Without going through this period where God builds your character

You will live out your calling only to fall, lose yourself and shame the name of the Lord.

You will get the dream job only to lose your fellowship with God.

You will marry only to separate and divorce.

You will get the next gig only to lose yourself.

You will find your spouse only to lead a miserable and depressing life.

You will launch your business only to the destruction of your inner self and joy.

In this period of waiting, God is building you up so you can sustain whatever it might be you're praying for or He is calling you to do in the long-term. God is not delaying anything. God is building a foundation that will withstand the storms.

BLESSED TO LAST

Joseph is a good example of someone who was blessed to last. His character was always solid. He always stood on what was right, regardless of circumstances. We see this when he turns down Potiphar's wife, when she attempts to make Joseph her side lover.

Joseph first received the dream of what God was calling him to do when he was seventeen years old. He told his brothers and dad about his dream. They all weren't happy with the idea that he shall reign over all of them. Imagine being seventeen and knowing your calling and being so sure of it. Then your brothers sell you and you become a slave in a foreign country. Joseph gets there, starts at the bottom but because he moves with the favor of God, he climbs up fast. The Bible says: "The Lord was with Joseph, and he was a successful man; and he was in the house of his master the Egyptian. And his master saw that the Lord was with him and that the Lord made all he did to prosper in his hand. So Joseph found favor in his sight, and served him. Then he made him overseer of his house, and all that he had he put under his authority" (Genesis 39:2-4).

Joseph received the call when he was seventeen. He was the beloved child of Israel; a man called by God to establish a nation for his people. But now, Joseph finds himself in the process. Slavery is definitely not his idea of the process he would go through to get to his destiny. But the Word says the Lord was with Joseph. And He was using this period to build the character of Joseph. Everything that happened to Joseph was meant to purify His character. So he can contain the responsibility that came with the blessings God had for him.

Just when things were getting better with his new promotion, his boss's wife wants a piece of him. Joseph saw this as a great opportunity to please God. He declared that he still believes that God was with him even in the reality he was living in. He cannot do such an evil thing before his God. This response was a great act of worship to God. This showed great character in Joseph. Potiphar's wife didn't take the rejection very well. She accuses him of trying to rape her. Joseph gets thrown in jail. But even in prison, he was a man of integrity and character. His attitude through everything he went through was directed as worship towards God.

Everyone who knew him knew he was a man of God. He refused to worship their gods and remained true to Jehovah. And it is evident that Joseph was in consistent fellowship with God. He pursued God. He chose God every time he was tested. From Potiphar's wife to when his brothers came to buy food in Egypt. God was personal to Him. It's from this he got the wisdom and strength to choose the Godly thing.

Joseph spends thirteen years of his life in the process. From the time when he received the call to when he was appointed governor over Egypt, his character was built and tested many times. His calling required a lot of character and God used the process to purify his character, so when the calling and dream is manifested, the blessing will last and God will be glorified. God was glorified when Joseph extended grace to his brothers. God was glorified when he saved the nation of Israel from famine, thus His promise to Abraham lived on. The God of Joseph was glorified for saving Egypt and the world.

TIME CONSCIOUS

It is so hard to comprehend the reality of eternity. Half the time I think I get it. Then when I hear myself say things like, "Yes, we'll be with God till the end of time" I realize I don't fully understand this concept of not having an end, of not having a finish line.

This has exposed my mentality. I think within the limitations of time. Time is essential to me. And to make things worse, me is essential to me. This self-based attitude of 'me' is what leads to a lot of chaos in one's life. Because we are running out of time, we are not getting any younger, and life is passing us by, we want things done and done in our time. We are not interested in long-term impact that glorifies God. We are consumed by the desire to feel good about ourselves because of our achievement. We don't fully understand the concept of "built to last" or rather "blessed to last". We want to skip from calling to manifestation. We want to skip from prayer to manifestation. We want to skip from God's promise to His manifestation of the promise. We are time conscious. We are forgetting that character is built with time. It's not overnight. There are no express factories producing character. It takes time.

We need to realize that everything good happens in God's time. And I say this knowing that, even the times we fall short during the process, He will use it for our own good. How great is our God? His Word says, "For the vision is yet for the appointed [future] time it hurries toward the goal [of fulfillment]; it will not fail. Even though it delays, wait [patiently] for it, Because it will certainly come; it will not delay" (Habakkuk 2:3, AMP).

GOD'S TIME IS THE BEST TIME

The phrase God's time is the best time is best illustrated through the life of Moses.

Moses as a Prince

Moses was born in a crazy time in Egypt. Pharaoh had issued a decree to kill all Hebrew newborn boys. So when Moses was born his mother hid him, but as he grew she decided to build a basket and send him off. Pharaoh's daughter then picked him up, and he was raised as a prince in the palace.

God knew Moses was the person He chose to deliver his people from

Egypt. It was no accident that Moses ended up in the palace. If Moses was going to be a deliverer, he needed to know what freedom is. If he was going to lead the whole nation from captivity, he needed to be trained in the best leadership school available. He also had to be accustomed with Pharaoh; he needed to know how to speak the king's language.

Moses as a Shepherd

God knew that the children of Israel don't know freedom. He knew they would be stubborn. He knew they will want to turn back and go to Egypt many times. He knew they would question Moses's authority and leadership many times. And God used forty years in the desert of the country of the Midians training Moses on patience doing a monotonous job, tending sheep for forty years. Sheep are dumb animals; they are stubborn animals. Moses shepherded them for forty years. Without the forty years in the wilderness, who knows what Moses would have done to the Israelites during their many doubtful times and when they deserted God. I mean, you've seen his temper, need I say more?

Moses on his Call

By the time God shows up at the burning bush, Moses is ready. He is built for impact. He is prepared for long-term impact. He is ready to do what God has called him to do. He has the royal leadership training, he knows how to lead a nation, and he has been trained on patience and leading stubborn, unstable and dumb creatures. By the time his call is manifested, Moses was ready for impact. We read of Moses to this day. Moses spent 80 years being trained for the call God had on his life.

God could have simply called Moses to deliver the Israelites after Moses killed the Egyptian, or before that. After all, Moses was trained to lead a nation, the most powerful nation in the world at the time. So he had the skills and gifts to carry out the call. But God is not just interested in gifts and skills to get the task done. He is more interested in character that will glorify Him and depend on Him throughout. He is a God of long-term impact and subduing, not instant results.

God is the one who called you. Only He knows what you need to fulfill the call on your life. Only He knows where to plant you to equip you for what you will need to glorify Him where He is calling you. Only He will decide when you're ready. The process is a time that God is building your character up so you can have long term impact, bringing Him glory where He is taking you. So you can be a powerful subduing part in the body of Christ.

the prize of the pro- **cess** *the prize of the* process **the prize of the process** *the prize of the process* **the prize of the process** *the prize of the pro-* cess **the prize of the process** *the prize of the process* **the prize of the process** *the prize of the* process **the prize of the process** *the prize of the process* **the prize of the process** *the prize of the process* **the prize of the pro-** **cess** *the prize of the* process **the prize of th**

Becoming like Jesus

08

{ACT 3}
THE PRIZE OF THE PROCESS

Conformity to Christlikeness

God uses the process to reveal who we truly are, so He can replace it with Christlikeness. I call this process the Christ-like transplant surgery. A transplant is only needed when an organ is failing. To become Christ-like, something in you must be failing. Thus the phrase, "in my weakness He is made strong." When I am weak, I make room to become like Him. So weakness is strength, if you allow Him to enter in and perform spiritual surgery. The waiting period allows you to realize your spiritual bankruptcy, so you can invite Him to do a transplant. John Bevere said it well in his book, Victory in the Wilderness, "Welcome His refining that you might be a vessel of honor, able to manifest His glory" (71).

The process is a period God uses to purge away our old dead self and conform us into the image of Christ. The season you are in right now is a rich season. Make the most out of it. Becoming like Christ is the ultimate goal of our growth as born again Christians. There is no better time to grow into Christlikeness than when we are in the process. Embrace it. Enjoy it. Stop complaining. Start becoming.

CONFORMITY TO CHRISTLIKENESS

God's perfect will for your life is for you to be conformed to the image of Christ. Christ is the perfect and only model of who we need to become. God uses the process to transform us into the image of Christ Jesus. When you decide to live your life with conformity to Christ-likeness as your utmost goal, everything is bearable.

The wilderness is bearable

The waiting is bearable

Pain is bearable

Confusion is bearable

You won't see the beauty of becoming like Christ until you get to know Christ. You won't see why God's perfect will for you is conformity to the image of Christ until you know who Christ is. If you take time to think about Jesus, you will realize He holds a depth that none of us can fully comprehend. This will probably be the hardest chapter I'll ever have to write. Christ holds such a depth that every author in the whole world can dedicate their entire career writing volumes about Jesus and we still won't cover His fullness. So I'll just pick very few things to bring this chapter into context.

Jesus is the only person who lived here on earth for thirty three years yet managed to have the biggest impact. His impact rings to eternity. His impact has saved and redeemed billions of people. How does a person do that? How do you live such an impactful life here on earth yet heavily invested in eternal rewards? And all He had was thirty three years.

The life Jesus lived is exactly the life God had predestined Him to live. He was always in fellowship with the Father. He was always in touch with the Holy Spirit. He was always at the right place at the right time doing the right thing. Jesus finished everything He was sent to do. His entire life was full of purpose. No time wasted. Jesus never wasted time doing things He had no business doing. He was all about doing the will of the Father. Regardless of what this meant for Him. Regardless of what this took from Him. He was in total obedience to the Father. He always operated from the realm of God. Every place He stepped into, He brought Heaven down. He changed atmospheres. He had no business pleasing men; He was in the business of pleasing the Father. He only said and did what the Father did and said. He was not influenced by the world. He influenced the world. He didn't care about impressing men; all He wanted was to be faithful to God. He loved God with His heart, soul and mind. All He wanted was to glorify the Father. He loved His neighbors as He loves Himself. He had a pure heart. He was meek. He was gentle. He was humble. He put others before Himself. He displayed the heart of the Father to those around Him. He lived a full life, a complete life. Not on His own terms, but God's. Glory to Christ Jesus!

This is what God wants us to become. His desire and will is for us to become like Christ Jesus. He is the model of what all God's children should become. So how and when does this happen? Paul answers this question with a verse of scripture that is widely used and mostly misused.

"And we know that all things work together for good to those who love God, to those who are called according to His purpose. For Whom He foreknew, He also *predestined to be conformed to the image of His Son* , that He might be the firstborn among many brethren" (Romans 8:28-29).

BEN OWDENsegment>

The context of verse 28 is found in verse 29. We have mostly used this verse suggesting that everything will work out for our comfort and desires. We have misused the word good, as used here, to mean prosperity, a quick fix, success and happiness. But the good that is mentioned in this verse refers to becoming like Christ. Your ultimate good is becoming like Christ. God is going to use every experience you go through, every season of your life, to conform you to the image of His Son. God uses the process heavily to conform us into the image of Christ. Every time you are in the process, you are giving God an opportunity to conform you to the image of Christ. So that who Christ is, you will become. This is your ultimate good.

In the process, you meet God's utmost desire, worship
In the process, you become what God desires, Christ-like

The process is a rich season for you to become Christ-like. Without the process, it'll always be more of you and less of Him. To glorify God in your calling, you must be Christ-like. To glorify God with the manifestation of your dream, you need to be Christ-like. To glorify God where He is taking you, you need to be Christ-like. To fulfill all that God has for your life, you must be Christ-like. My dream in this life is to die empty. To fulfill all that God has predestined for me. Without being Christ-like, this is a pipe dream. Christ is the model for fulfilling purpose and destiny. My dream for you is that at the end of your life, you say, "I have run the race, I have finished the task, I have kept the faith"

Without being Christ-like;
You will not reach your destiny.
You will not subdue the earth.

78

You will not glorify God with your victories.

You will not fulfill your God-given dreams.

You will miss your breakthrough.

The process should be your favorite season. In fact, it needs to be. Without it, there is nothing but trouble. Are you becoming Christ-like or Christless? You are in the richest season of your life. The decision to dig the riches that lay beneath this season is up to you. What's it going to be?

FOOD FOR THE CHRIST-LIKE

One of the most earth shattering things Jesus has ever said was "My food is to do the will of Him who sent Me, and to finish His work" (John 4:34). This is one of my favorite verses of scripture. It's a scripture I live by. To understand this punch line we must understand the prelude of this moment. Jesus had been on a journey from Judea to Galilee but passing through Samaria. The mode of transportation at the time was mainly walking. When He reached Jacob's well in Samaria, Jesus was weary and hungry. So He rests by the well while His disciples go to buy food. While resting, the woman we know today as the Samaritan woman shows up. Jesus ministers to her. By the time the disciples come back, Jesus felt like He had just finished dipping chapatis in a bowl of beans with a bottle of coke. He is nourished. The disciples urge Him "Rabbi, eat" But Jesus said to them, "I have food to eat of which you do not know" (John 4:32). "Wait, what? You have food? Then why did you allow us to go and find you food?" This is how I would've responded to Jesus, but while the disciples were wondering who gave Jesus food, Jesus said to them, "My food is to do the will of Him who sent Me, and to finish His work."

This verse of scripture is one of the most beautiful displays of the heart of Christ. It shows what lies in the core of the heart of Jesus. Jesus found nourishment and satisfaction in doing the will of the Father. He didn't maintain life and growth by eating and servicing his flesh. But by doing the will of God and finishing what God has called Him to do. This revelation is the epicenter of Christlikeness.

Oxford English Dictionary defines food as any nutritious substance that people or animals eat or drink or that plants absorb *in order to maintain life and growth* .

Doing the will of the Father is monumental for the Christ-like. In doing the will of God they maintain life and growth. Let me bring this into focus. I have never met anyone in this life who gave up on food. Never have I heard of someone who thought food was too much work and she or he gave up eating. No human being gives up on food. Even those who are clinically ill and can't put their hands to their mouth eat through tubes. Now, what food is to the body, doing the will of the Father is to the Christ-like. They never give up on doing the will of the Father. Giving this up is equivalent to giving up on food. It's the same as starving yourself to death. You want to know why Paul persevered with joy amidst all the suffering the gospel brought him? He was Christ-like. Fulfilling God's call on his life was like food for him. He couldn't give up on it. Regardless of what it brought. Regardless of what it took. Regardless of what it meant. This is the spirit and the heart of the Christ-like.

The Christ-like

His diet is the will of God

Fulfilling it is quenching his hunger

Emptying his plate

He waits on the Lord with patience

Fervently sticks on the path

To him the will of God is like breath

Without it, there's vacuum and death

In it he is nourished, he progresses his health

His life and growth is enhanced

His perseverance is perfected

After all, he is a foodie

Who joys in emptying his plate

One who is Christ-like doesn't find nourishment in comfort and plea-sure. They find it in doing the will of our Lord Christ Jesus. It's fulfilling their God given dreams. It's responding to God's call on their life. It's finishing what God has called them to do. It's manifesting heaven here on earth. This is how they maintain life and growth. Anything short of God's will is a slow, painful death for them. What is the will of God in your situation? What is the will of the Father in your process?

Is it to keep your faith?

Is it to be a faithful steward?

Is it to step into the unknown?

Is it to worship Him in your confusion?

Is it to serve others faithfully?

Is it to encourage others while you're confused?

Is it to love unconditionally those blocking your success?

Is it to extend grace and mercy to those destroying you?

The cross was no joke, but Jesus found nourishment in fulfilling God's call on His life. No matter the cost. The pain. The suffering. This is the test of Christ-likeness. This is who God wants you to become. The process is a time God uses to transform you into a place where your food is to do His will for your life. No matter the cost. No matter how long it takes. No matter what it takes from you!

THE MOTIVE FOR THE CHRIST-LIKE

What motivates the Christlike is love and what they want to attain is love. Jesus said, the greatest commandments are loving God and loving your neighbor. His point being, everything hangs on love: love for God and love for your neighbor. We have covered the loving God part, now let's look at the loving others part.

In his most well known chapter, Paul writes, "If I have the gift of prophecy and can fathom all mysteries and all knowledge, and *if I have a faith that can move mountains* , but do not have love, I am nothing. If I give all I possess to the poor and give over my body to hardship that I may boast, but do not have love, I gain nothing" (1 Corinthians 13:2-3, NIV). Later Paul adds on, "Let all that you do be done in love" (1 Corinthians 16:14, ESV). Bringing everything full circle. Anything you do without love is pretty much like vapor. Anything you do without the pure motive of love is meaningless to God. He won't reward you for it; He won't bless you for it. If the motivation is not love, you are wasting your effort, time and resources. And this is especially true about your calling and dreams. If you are not pursuing them with the pure motive of love, you wont gain anything of eternal value after fulfilling them. And the Bible explicitly says, you can have the greatest gift of faith but if you don't have love, then it's all for nothing. If there is no love, you can move mountains and part seas, but it won't mean a thing.

It's for this reason God is keeping you in the process. He is using the process to purify your motive. Molding your motive into love. He loves you too much to sit aside and watch you waste your life away by working hard knowing that you are not attaining anything of eternal value. Let me bring this into context. Jesus said, love your neighbor as I have loved you. We have watered this down to being there for people, especially when they need to talk to someone, making time to have coffee with people, and texting and calling. Don't get me wrong, these are good things to do and they do express love, but the love Jesus was talking about is far bigger and greater than this. He didn't just love us by simply having coffee with us, or texting and calling us and being there for us when we need Him. Now, He does all these things and more for us, maybe not coffee, unless you had coffee with Him. But His greatest expression of love was choosing to leave Heaven in obedience to the Father to come and offer His life as a ransom for ours. His greatest expression of love was giving humanity what only He could give, eternal life. The same applies to you. Your greatest expression of love is giving humanity what only you could give, the purpose God has laid upon your life, the God given dreams He has given you or as some would say, His call on your life. This is your greatest expression of love to your neighbors. So failing at following God's call on your life is failing to love your neighbor. Quitting on your God given dreams is quitting to love your neighbor. You are not quitting on a dream but on love. You are not failing at a calling but at love.

God is using the process to purify your motive from self-centered, ego boosting motives to motives centered on pure love. Why should your motive be love? The bible says it more clearly, "Love never fails" (1 Corinthians 13:8). When your motive is love, you will not fail, you will not quit. Jesus's motive was love, that's why He never failed and He never quit. He fulfilled the greatest commandments. He loved God and He loved His neighbor. Some of us fail and quit because the motive is not love, the motive is to get glory, to secure our futures, to make money, to leave a legacy, to be happy, to live a meaningful life, to feel like we matter and all these will fail, only love will prevail.

When the motive is love you realize that quitting on that business God called you to start means robbing your neighbor a job opportunity where they will be equipped to feed their families and be a blessing to their community. And love does not rob its neighbors. When the motive is love you realize that quitting to write that book is robbing your neighbor the knowledge that will scale them to the next level where they will thrive and prosper. And love does not rob its neighbors. When the motive is love you realize that quitting on the music God called you to create is robbing your neighbor the hope, encouragement and inspiration that will take them through a hard time. And love does not rob its neighbors. When the motive is love you will realize that quitting on the films God called you to produce, write or direct is robbing your neighbor the hope, encouragement and inspiration that will champion them through a hard time. And love does not rob its neighbors. I could write a whole chapter of these scenarios, but I am sure by now you get the gist of it. Love never fails, and when love is your motive, you will never fail. That's why God is keeping you in the process to purify your motive so you don't fail where He is calling you. He is also keeping you in the process to purify your motive so you don't waste your life living your dreams and your calling but losing your eternal rewards. Love is the motive for the Christlike. Love is the reason we chase our dreams and it's the reason we don't quit. Is love the motive for chasing your dreams? Is love the motive for starting that business, writing that book, going into ministry, making that record, going for that job? Is love the motive? If not, invite Him to purify your motives.

THE ONLY CONSTANT FOR THE CHRIST-LIKE

What is the most constant thing in your life? What is the one thing you do consistently above all else? Is it eating? Is it working? Is it entertainment? What is the most constant thing in your life? Think about it!

To the Christ-like, God is infinite so pursuing Him is the only constant. This is their utmost priority in life. Communing with their Abba, their Lord God, their hope and joy. How good is it to be like Christ?

Christ Jesus did this so well that the disciples asked Him to teach them how to pray. His fellowship with God was His utmost priority. No circumstance hindered His fellowship. Even when He was about to be crucified, He spent His longest recorded prayer time at the garden of Gethsemane. He often got out of busy days to go spend personal time with God. Everything He did flowed from His fellowship with the Father. He was hungry and thirsty for more of God. This is the only constant for the Christ-like. Seeking more of God. The process is a beautiful time to seek more of God. The Christ-like thrives with more of God. Fellowship always comes first to them. As long as they are in fellowship with the Lord, they have all they need. David said this of his thirst for God:

"As the deer pants [longingly] for the water brooks, So my [a]soul pants [longingly] for You, O God. My soul (my life, my inner self) thirsts for God, for the living God. When will I come and see the face of God?" (Psalm 42:1-2, AMP).

Animals don't have as many luxuries as we do. In fact, the only luxury they have is the absence of jobs and employment systems. They live very simple lives. But this simplicity of lifestyle is overshadowed by the complexity of diversity in their species. Deer's in particular are very unique and interesting animals. They need water more than anything. Majority of the food they eat contain up to eighty percent water. Water nourishes a deer. It is a necessity.

This crazy love for water has made it easy to hunt deers. Build a fake pond and deers will show up. The deer doesn't end up at the stream by accident. The deer is intentional about finding a stream. They live for the water brook.

The more you look into this illustration, the more you realize why the psalmist used it to explain his thirst for more of God. Deers live for that sip by the water stream. They dance with joy upon finding it. This is the spirit of the Christ-like. They pant for more of God. They don't stop until they get more of Him. They always want more of God. The infinity and eternal nature of God makes their panting ceaseless and consistent to eternity.

Pursue His presence

All the time

Bring Heaven down

His kingdom come

His will be done

On earth, as it is in Heaven

You can't bring what you don't know

You can't know what you don't pursue

How bad do you want more of God?

How bad do you want more of His Spirit?

Like Paul who considered everything rubbish

Compared to knowing Christ

Like David who yearned for God

Like a deer pants for the brook

Seek the Lord and His strength

Seek His presence continually

This is the only constant for the Christ-like

God is infinite. God is eternal. God is so big and deep that no created being can fully know Him. The tragedy is that while there is an infinite God waiting for us to pursue Him relentlessly, we are too busy being content with our current experience of Him.

God has graced you with the process so you can focus on pursuing Him above all else. So you can learn to elevate your pursuit of Him above your pursuit of dreams and breakthroughs. Fellowship with God is the primary thing in all of life. God wants to show you more of Him; He wants you to see His beauty, to hear His voice, to feel His touch, to smell His scent, to enjoy Him. To fully enjoy where He is taking you, you need to first learn how to enjoy Him above all else. He wants to take you to a place where He is all that you need. He is using the process to take you there. There is no better time to really see if He is all you need than when you are in the process. The wilderness revealed that the Israelites needed comfort more than they needed God. Do you want your dreams to come true more than you want more of God? Do you want to live out your calling more than you want more of God? Do you want your breakthrough more than you want more of God?

As the deer pants for the brook

So I pant for you oh Lord

Immersed in joy and excitement

I draw close to you oh Jesus

As the deer is nourished by the water

I find nourishment in your presence

As the deer lives for the quenching by the stream

I also live for the quenching found in your presence

As the deer longs for the sweet taste of the spring

I long to see and taste how good You are

Complete joy for the Christ-like

Joy is the quest of mankind. We are all searching for joy. I have come to believe that what you elect as the source of your joy will determine your level of endurance in the process. If you elect fulfilled dreams and answered prayers as sources of your joy, you won't endure the process. If you elect the pleasure that comes with your God-sized dreams as a source of joy then you won't persevere the process. You need to elect something concrete. You need a source of joy that can weather any storm. Thankfully, Jesus points us to the source of this kind of joy.

"As the Father loved Me, I also have loved you; abide in My love. If you keep My commandments, you will abide in My love, just as I have kept My Father's commandments and abide in His love. "These things I have spoken to you, that My joy may remain in you, and *that* your joy may be full" (John 15:9-11).

"Christ loves believers unconditionally. But as believers obey Christ's Word and abide in His love, they come to experience and understand His love for them more and more, [and it's in this believer's experience] of Christ's love, [they experience] complete Joy" (NKJV Study Bible).

In John 15, Jesus reveals a kingdom principle that meets this consuming human need for joy. He meets this need and then some. He offers fulfilled joy.

The Father's love for Jesus is not at the top of our topics of interest. God's love for Jesus comes up when we are trying to understand how much He loves us to a point of sacrificing His only begotten Son. Aside from this, it's not really much of our concern; you don't come across sermons or books titled "Jesus is loved by His Dad."

God is our Abba. Until we are able to trace everything back to Him, we won't understand the mysteries of this life. It all starts with the Father loving Jesus. This is the first door. And as the Father has loved Jesus, Jesus also loves us. This is the second door.

The love of the Father towards Jesus is a perfect love. It's unconditional in its nature. Jesus and the Father are one so the Father's love knows no boundaries. It's a love that has always known intimacy and oneness. It unites the Father and His beloved Son for all eternity. This is how deep His love for Jesus runs. This love is characterized by trust and submission. God created everything through Jesus and for Jesus. It's a love that doesn't hold back.

Jesus uses the love of the Father to Him as the setup for His love for us. As the Father has loved Him, He also loves us. His love for us is as unconditional as the Father's love is for Him. His love for us doesn't hold back just as much as His Father's love for Him doesn't hold back. His love for us is consuming, empowering and unconditional.

I know you're wondering what's all this got to do with joy? Well, this was the backdrop Jesus laid out before He got to His punch line, so it's important we don't miss it. After painting a picture of His love for us, He then gives a command. He says "abide in My love." This is the third and final door. Jesus is not talking about theology, He is sharing a Kingdom secret that He has been applying before time began. The words "Abide in My love" are the keys to unlock this complete joy found in the heart of God's unconditional love.

But the words "abide in My love" sound like encrypted spy language. So let's break it down. How do we abide in His love? His next Words answer that: "If you keep My commandments, you will abide in My love." Simply put, we abide in His love by obeying Him and His Word. To make it simpler, we abide in His love by loving Him in the way He wants to be loved, in obedience. This makes obedience to the Lord the pathway to experience the fullness of His unconditional love for us. What was the point of Jesus revealing this Kingdom principle? Verse 11 wraps it up. "These things I have spoken to you, that My joy may remain in you, and that your joy may be full."

This is God's design for fulfilled joy. This is the same path Jesus takes to experience His fulfilled joy, by abiding in His Father's love. So my dear friend, you can't redesign God's blueprint for fulfilled joy. Quit trying. Submit to His design and experience fulfilled joy. Why am I strongly emphasizing joy? Without it, you won't endure the process. You'll quit when the going gets tougher.

We spend so much money and time, we go to extreme lengths, just to experience joy. Joy is the quest of man. We pursue dreams hoping to find joy. We decide to pursue our callings hoping to find joy. We pursue pleasure and relationships hoping to find joy. Most of us do what we do so we can have joy. Most of us live all of our lives experiencing incomplete joy because we seek it in the wrong places.

God is our creator. He has engineered in us a device I like to call Joy Compatibility. Every human being has this engineered inside of his or her being. This device is only compatible with God. This is the way it works. Everything else is incompatible with it. The Christlike know and believe this and they quit pursuing joy elsewhere. They know it's a waste of time and energy. They know they can't reprogram what God has engineered. It's mission impossible.

Jesus is not a means to our joy; He is the fulfillment of our joy. No amount of money, power, influence, family and friends will fulfill your joy. We always make the mistake of using Christ as a means to get to these things, thinking that they are the fulfillment of our joy - we are wrong. Christ is the fulfillment of our joy and only when His love abides in us and we abide in Him, do we experience complete joy, joy that surpasses all understanding. The Christlike live their lives embodying this truth. Believing it. Applying it.

In the process, you meet God's utmost desire, worship

In the process, you become what God desires, Christ-like

In the process, you bring Him what He is worthy of, Glory

In the process, you experience what God desires for you, full joy

Fulfilled and complete joy is found in the unconditional love of Christ. It's yours to experience. All you have to do is love God through your obedience, obey what God is instructing you to do in your process. No matter how painful or embarrassing it might feel like. The Christ-like finds joy in loving God. Like how Jesus loved His Father by obeying Him to the point of the cross. This is how you experience joy in the process.

The bar of joy has been raised. Are you going to settle to the lesser or the great? Now don't get me wrong, I am not saying we are cutting deals with God. I'll give you my obedience and you give me joy. This approach is selfish and doesn't bring glory to God. Thus forfeiting fulfilled joy. All I am saying is simply this; fulfilled joy is a fruit of obedience. You need joy to endure the process. You need obedience to endure the process.

THE WEIGHT OF HIS GLORY

For great is the LORD and greatly to be praised; He is to be feared above all gods. For all the gods of the peoples are idols, But the LORD made the heavens. Splendor and majesty are before Him, Strength and beauty are in His sanctuary. Ascribe to the LORD, O families of the peoples, Ascribe to the LORD glory and strength. Ascribe to the LORD the glory of His name; Bring an offering and come into His courts. Worship the LORD in holy attire; Tremble before Him, all the earth (Psalm 96:4-9, ESV).

The word glory is a word we use a lot on a regular basis. Glory to God has been a phrase that easily rolls off the tongue. The word as used in the Bible originates from the Hebrew word Kâbôd which means to be heavy; in the good sense of abundant or copious. Glorifying God is declaring and attesting the depth of the nature of who God is. Declaring and attesting the heaviness of who He is, that there is none like Him, that He owns everything you have, that He is ever faithful, ever good, ever loving and that He never fails and so forth. This is the essence of glorifying God. Anything we do or say that doesn't attest to His true nature can't possibly bring glory to Him.

Yet, we often say things like, 'It's all for the glory of God" or "Glory to God" very lightly. But the things we attach to His glory (the depth of His true nature) sometimes represent the opposite. At the end of His earthly ministry, Jesus said, "I glorified You on the earth, having accomplished the work which You have given Me to do." (John 17:4, ESV). The entire life of Jesus was dedicated to declaring and attesting to the true nature of His Father, and through Jesus we saw the true nature of the Father. That He is loving, good, kind, compassionate, that He is Lord over everything and everyone. In fact, at one point Jesus said, "I don't speak on my own authority. The Father who sent me has commanded me what to say and how to say it" (John 12:49, NLT).

The entire life of Jesus is the blueprint of how we should live our lives. This is what being Christ-like means. Having the attitude, priorities, thoughts, words, actions and reactions of Jesus. Dedicated to declaring and attesting the true nature of our Father to the world around us.

Sometimes we forget that Jesus spent the longest time in the waiting period, more than anybody else. He spent more than 3000 years waiting for his incarnate birth. No one has ever done it better than Jesus. He glorified the Father from when He was called to when He was resurrected. He glorified God in the mundane and the glorious. He glorified God in the painful and the joyful. He glorified God in public and in private. He glorified God in the light and in the dark. Through Jesus we see and know that God is the same, yesterday, today and forever. He is consistent. He attested the same nature of God on the cross, and when He fed the five thousand. Does your life attest to the consistent and true nature of God at all seasons of your life? Or do people think God is inconsistent when they look at your life?

Jesus glorified His Father by how He lived His life every single day. Are you glorifying your Father by how you are living your life in the process? Are you as joyful and content in the process as much as you would be when God answers your prayers and makes you prosperous? Are you praising God in the process as much as you would when He grants your dreams? Is the nature of God the same to you in the process as it is at the manifestation of your prayers and dreams? Are you attesting to the Heaviness and the glorious nature of our Father, Lord and Saviour and His Spirit that lives inside of us through your life in the process?

With:

Your thoughts

Your actions

Your reactions

Do they attest to the Spirit of God in you?

Your intentions

Your motives

Do they attest to the holiness of God?

Your faith

Your stewardship

Does it attest to the faithfulness of God?

Aspiring to be Christ-like is aspiring to live a life that glorifies the Triune God. When I read the Bible and see how David trembled before God, how he was all about bringing glory to the Father, I become challenged. David lived in the most blessed time in the Old Testament than any other, because it was during David's reign that we learn of David's Tabernacle, which is the Ark of the Covenant that carried the presence of God. During David's reign it didn't have the veil of the temple separating the Holy of Holies from the outer court and the middle court. People had access to what previously was exclusive to the high priest. This meant people could worship joyfully and freely. That's why when you read the Psalms, David is drunk with the presence of God. This was a prophetic era because it foretold the experience that will be available for all who believe in Christ Jesus, the descendant of David.

It's quite hard to glorify God when His glory and majesty is evident to us only in theory. Pure glory stems from pressing into the Holy of Holies and experiencing the glorious presence of the living God that you say, "One thing I have desired of the Lord, That will I seek: That I may dwell in the house of the Lord All the days of my life, To behold the beauty of the Lord, And to inquire in His temple" (Psalm 27:4).

We are only able to glorify God and live a life that glorifies Him when we know Him. When we experience Him and all the joys of His presence. This way, our submission and obedience stems from our love for God and not works.

The command to bring glory to God can often seem like a setup to fail. But when we pursue God, we become equipped to glorify Him. How does the pursuit of God equip me to glorify God? You might ask. Jesus revealed a great Kingdom principle when He said, "Seek first the Kingdom of God and His righteousness and all these things shall be added unto you." The context of what He was saying was material needs but what He was revealing is a Kingdom principle. When you pursue God above all else, He will provide for your needs. And if what you need is an increase in ability and capacity to glorify Him, He will meet that need.

When we pursue the depth of God,

Our capacity to glorify Him will be increased.

Our capacity to worship Him will be increased.

Our capacity to trust Him will be increased.

Our capacity to persevere will be increased.

Our capacity to endure will be increased.

Our capacity to be meek will be increased.

Our capacity to wait in His time will be increased.

Our capacity to submit unto Him will be increased.

THE MIND OF THE CHRIST-LIKE

The state of your mind will determine a lot of things about your life. Who you are is dependent upon what you think. "As a man thinketh in his heart, so is he" (Proverbs 23:7, KJV). There are a lot of philosophies about the mind in the world today. The most popular being positive thinking. The truth is by now you have realized this can only take you so far. It can't take you through everything. In fact, positive thinking can even take you away from God's will, because not everything positive is Godly.

Positive thinking won't take you through persecution. Positive thinking won't take you through the most confusing and painful times of your life in a way that glorifies God. If Jesus were a "positive thinker" He wouldn't have made it to the cross. Positive thinking has it's basis attached to this world. It's woven into this world, conformed to this world. Positive thinking is not the mind of Christ. It's a man-made coping mechanism.

The mind of the Christ-like is a transformed mind. It is a renewed mind. Detached from the patterns of this world and conformed to the mind of Christ Jesus. This is a mind that will get you through any process you will go through in this life.

I can't talk about the transformation of the mind without going to Romans 12:2. This verse of scripture is known to identify the need for the transformation of the mind. "And do not be conformed to this world, but *be transformed* by *the renewing of your mind* that you *may prove* what is that good and acceptable and *perfect will of God.*"

I love this scripture, mainly because it points back to God's perfect will for us. Becoming like Christ. The goal of a renewed mind is so we can think like Jesus. When we think like Jesus we become like Christ. The end of which is glorifying God through anything and everything. Become one with God. Honoring our one line vow in the covenant we have with Him. Offering Him the purest form of worship, worshipping Him both in truth and in spirit. And let's be honest, most times this life doesn't appear to be positive. Abiding with God's stand on issues like homosexuality and divorce requires a renewed mind, the mind of Christ, not a positive mind, because let's face it, you can find positivity in same sex marriage and divorce.

The only way to attain the mind of Christ is through His Word abiding in you. And His word says:

"If then you were raised with Christ, *seek those things which are above, where Christ is*, sitting at the right hand of God. *Set your mind on things above*, not on things on the earth" (Colossians 3:1-2).

A renewed mind seeks things that are above. After all, our job is to bring heaven down. How can we bring heaven down when we don't know it and we don't think like they think up there? His will be done, on earth as it is in heaven. Are you bringing heaven down into the midst of your process? Are you seeking the will of God in your process? Do you view the process as you see it or do you have a heavenly perspective concerning your process? Is your mindset where Christ is? Do you see the silence of God or do you see the glory of God in your process? Do you see the confusion in your process or do you see Christ in your process?

The end is the mind of Christ

The impact is proving the perfect will of God

The process is the renewal

The renewal happens in threefold

Detaching from the patterns of this world

Seeking things which are above, where Christ is

Setting your mind on things above

Where His glory abounds

Angels sing of His faithfulness

And Holy! Holy! Holy! Never ceases

The Christ-like can walk through anything and everything in this life and still glorify God and worship Him, for He is worthy and good. This is where God wants every believer to be. This is where God wants you to be. He is using the process to renew your mind. Giving you a Christ-like mind. So you can glorify God through anything and everything, both at the manifestation and the dry, painful and confusing times of the process.

the great discourage-ment *the great discour-agement* **the great discouragement** *the great discouragement* **the great discourage-ment** *the great discour-agement* **the great discouragement** *the great dis-couragement* **the great dis-couragement** *the great discourage-ment* **the great dis-couragement** *the great discouragement* **the great discourage-ment** *the great discour-agement* **the great discouragement** *the g*

when everything seems to fall apart

10

The great discouragement

What do you do when things go from bad to worse when you're in the process? Do you take it as a sign that God is not with you in the endeavor? Do you give up and move on to the next thing? Do you blame God for leading you this far? Or do you condemn yourself for believing in God in regards to that dream, that breakthrough, that miracle, and that calling? What do you do when things go from bad to worse when you're in the process?

Most of our processes involve things going from bad to worse. Just when you thought there would be progress, the breakthrough falls through. Just when you thought you saw light at the end of the tunnel, the light disappears like lightening, and darkness covers your peripheral. These are often the most painful and confusing times in one's process. A time when God is quiet while you need Him to speak the most. A time when you are tempted to feel like God has abandoned you. This is the darkest hour of the process. No story better illustrates the great discouragement like Joseph's (Genesis 37-41).

Joseph first received his God given dream at age seventeen (Genesis 37:5). The dream revealed that he would become a ruler, a fierce leader, and a leader even over his family. Like any dreamer, Joseph couldn't keep the dream to himself. He told his family and his brothers hated him even more. That hatred escalated to the thought of killing Joseph but instead they decided to sell him as a slave to Midianite traders. This is the first phase of going from good to worse for Joseph. He went from being the most beloved son of his father Jacob, from being the kid with the big God given dreams, to being a slave.

He gets to Egypt; the Ishmaelites sell him to Potiphar, an officer of Pharaoh, captain of the guard, a powerful guy in Egypt. Joseph is now a slave in a godless country. Further away from home where his dreams would come true. After all, the dream showed he would rule over his family, and his family was far from Egypt. And Egypt doesn't have precedence or policy of making foreign slaves rulers of their land. His dreams went from tight dreams to pipe dreams. Life officially got worse.

Then a glimmer of hope appears as he is faithfully serving in the house of Potiphar. He finds favor in the sight of his master. This was his up and up. Joseph rises to the top of the house. He becomes boss over Potiphar's house. God blesses everything Joseph touches in the house of Potiphar. This was not the Midas touch; it was God's touch. Potiphar goes from well off to really rich because of the favor of God on Joseph. This was suddenly a breakthrough with enormous potential. Maybe Joseph thought he could win over Potiphar. And Potiphar will choose to grant him freedom. Joseph would be free to go back home, where his dreams can come true. Things were starting to look up again.

The Bible says Joseph was handsome in form and appearance. In today's terminology, we can simply say, Joseph was hot. Now Potiphar's wife, who in today's terminology we would call a cougar, started casting longing eyes on Joseph. Incase you were wondering, this is biblical for wanting to get some.

She was a very thirsty woman. Joseph, being a man of integrity, turned her down, saying, he can't commit such wickedness and sin against God and it was not right to do that to his master. He got away, but only for a short while. The desires of Potiphar's wife increased and she couldn't control herself so she jumped and held on to Joseph's shirt saying the infamous thirsty people slogan, "Come to bed with me!" (Genesis 39:7, NIV). But Joseph, being a Godly man, ran for his life and went outside. I can almost hear the Spirit of God telling Joseph, "Run Joseph, Run Joseph, Run Joseph." A habit most of us should embody but we have left it in the hands of Forest Gump. Left embarrassed, embittered and angry, Potiphar's wife accuses Joseph of rape, and Joseph is thrown into prison. His breakthrough just fell through. His glimmer of hope just turned into darkness. The possibility of ever being a free man just turned into wishful thinking. His destiny could only stretch within the confinement of the prison walls. Again, things went from worse to worst.

THE SILVER LINING

Imagine being Joseph, your life being a series of bad to worse, worse to worst chain of events. What do you do? How do you perceive what's happening in this kind of process? To be honest, this is hard. His process was not the easiest journey. But in all that gloominess and darkness there was a silver lining. The Word of God says, "The LORD was with Joseph..." (Genesis 39:2). The Lord was with Joseph from the moment his brothers sold him. The Lord was with Joseph when he was a slave at Potiphar's house and that's why he prospered. When Joseph was unfairly sent to prison, the Word of God says, "But the LORD was with Joseph..." (Genesis 39:21) and Joseph found favor with the keeper of the prison and Joseph became boss over his fellow prisoners.

On the surface his life looked like it was going from bad to worse. His breakthroughs kept falling through. But the Lord was always with Him and

He made Joseph prosper wherever he landed. Things didn't go exactly how Joseph wanted but the Lord was with Him and He made him prosper. We have the same promise from God. When Jesus was ascending to Heaven, He said, "...I am with you always, even to the end of the age" (Matthew 28:20). In countless verses in the Bible God is telling you, "I am with you." What do you do when things go from bad to worse when you're in the process? You cling to His presence and you continue pursuing Him. The silver lining of Joseph's bad to worse process was the presence of the Lord in and over His life.

In your darkest hour of the process, the Lord is with you. In the most disappointing and confusing hour of your process the presence of the Lord is with you. This is all you need in such a time. Sadly sometimes it doesn't feel like this, but this is your silver lining. As long as the Lord is with you, you have all that you need. He will make you prosperous even in your darkest hour. This success may not necessarily be what you were expecting but God's ways are higher than our ways. Being a prosperous prisoner wasn't part of Joseph's plans to achieve his dreams. But that's the process the Lord used to get Joseph to his dream.

God may be making you prosper at fulfilling someone else's dream and breakthrough while yours seems to be dying. This could be the prosperity brought upon by the presence of God in the midst of waiting. God may impart joy in your life in times of great sorrow. This could be the prosperity brought upon by the presence of God in the midst of waiting. God may impart great hope in times of great barrenness and darkness. This could be the prosperity brought upon by the presence of God in the midst of waiting. God may impart strong zeal and perseverance in your life in times of great opposition. This could be the prosperity brought upon by the presence of God in the midst of waiting.

Open your eyes and see the silver lining in your darkest night.

11

The lie of the enemy

Satan is not mindful of the things of God. He doesn't know the mind of God nor does He know the heart of God. He is only mindful of destruction. He is a theif, a deceiver, and a killer. And on top of that, he is short sighted. He has a blurred vision. The enemy cannot lead you into anything good. He is consumed with himself that he cannot see anything outside of his interests nor is he able to. Heeding to his counsel is choosing to walk into absolute destruction. It's a highway to the slaughterhouse. His expertise is to lead you astray, where you go from there doesn't really matter, as long as you don't find your way back to God. He only knows how to get you lost. That's his mastery.

This means he doesn't understand why you are at a certain stage in your life and why you have to go through what you go through. He is not in the business of deciphering God's plans for your life. He is in the business of corrupting whatever God seems to be doing in your life and through your life. His goal is to corrupt and kill whatever good he can find in your life. Using your situation, which he doesn't understand, to his advantage. He will deceive you, corrupt you and jeopardize your mission. He can't decipher God's ways. It's beyond him. God says: "for just as the heavens are higher than the earth, so My ways are higher than your ways and My thoughts higher than your thoughts." (Isaiah 55:9, NLT) This means His ways are higher than the ways of every created being, including satan.

The devil couldn't decipher why God allowed Joseph's life to go from bad to worse. He probably thought that he was burying Joseph and his dreams. The enemy probably thought he was winning. But God allowed this to happen for His purposes.

The enemy will use your bad to worse situations to his advantage. He will talk you out of your breakthrough, your dream, your calling and your miracle when things go from bad to worse. Getting you lost is his expertise. We see this more clearly in the gospel of Matthew.

"From that time Jesus began to show to His disciples that He must go to Jerusalem, and suffer many things from the elders and chief priests and scribes, and be killed, and be raised again the third day. Then Peter took Him aside and began to rebuke Him, saying, "Far be it from You Lord; this shall not happen to You!" But He turned and said to Peter, *"Get behind Me, Satan! You are an offense to Me, for you are not mindful of the things of God, but the things of men* " (Matthew 16:21-23).

I love this scripture because it displays the short sightedness of the devil. Jesus was telling His disciples of His destiny, the cross. The cross was the predestined end of the human suffering and bondage to sin. The cross was the only way Jesus could end our eternal misery. He had to carry His cross. This destiny had no room for self. Then as He tells His disciples this, Peter, who was under the influence of satan at the time says, "Far be it from You Lord; this shall not happen to You!" (v. 22) On the surface this looks like a justified concern, how can you die Jesus? You are the Son of the Living God, the Messiah the world has been waiting for, just order angels to take care of the priests and scribes.

Jesus could have chosen to escape the cross; He had the power to not go through it. So Peter, under the influence of satan wasn't completely ludicrous rebuking Jesus. But if you look closely, this is the same method satan used to tempt Jesus in the wilderness. He wanted to get him lost. In the wilderness he wanted Jesus to worship Him and apostate, now he was trying to get him off the cross. To prove how short sighted he is, look at how he was using different people to do contradicting things. He used the scribes and Pharisees to plot the death of Jesus. Then He influenced Peter to talk Jesus out of falling into the same trap he is setting. What a conflict. How short sighted. Jesus knew this about satan. He sets him straight. Jesus is the true OG! Omniscience God. Jesus says, "Get behind me satan!" (v. 23). Some of us need to get into the habit of saying this, "Get behind me satan!"

He goes on to say, *"You are an offense to Me, for you are not mindful of the things of God, but the things of men."* Jesus knew the enemy is short sighted. He created him (as an angel before he chose to go rogue). The enemy doesn't know why sometimes God allows you to go from bad to worse. But he will try and use it to his agenda. He will use self as a way to manipulate you into walking away from your destiny. He will use comfort, pride, pleasure and all self-based vices to get you lost. He will use your darkest hour to talk you out of your dreams, calling and breakthrough. After all, "You are a child of God, why would you go through this?" "Jesus died so you can live a happy stress free life, this is not of God, run." "God is a good God, He wouldn't allow you to stay here this long, that was not His dream, it was all you, walk out, don't waste any more time." "God doesn't allow His children to suffer, check out now, this is not Him." The list of these lies goes on and on. Depending on your level of maturity, his tricks can go up to two levels deep. There are probably more levels, but they are beyond my knowledge. I only know in part.

The enemy knows the power of God that dwells in you. The enemy knows what's going to happen when you die to self and allow God to work in you and through you in your process. The enemy knows that under the new covenant you are not one to play with. The enemy knows that you are free and your freedom will impact this world for the glory of God. He knows that God has a purpose for your life. He knows that when we all live free of ALL self, sin, fear and shame, the light that will shine in this world will be as bright as the sun. He knows that it will be on earth as it is in Heaven. To stop this from happening he keeps persuading us to resurrect the former self. Blinding you in your process and blurring your vision. Stalling you from living out your new reality. He manages to blind and stall some people till their time is up. Many have died this way. They missed their miracles, their breakthroughs, their dreams, their calling, and their destiny. They heeded to the counsel of a shortsighted visionless deceiving self-centered evil creature.

Let me paint a picture for you. Jesus comes down from Heaven, lives as a sinless Man and He dies at the cross. Carrying all our transgressions, paying the price for our sin. He dies at the cross, and He says, "It is finished" (John 19:30), boom, freedom is unleashed, and freedom is now a reality for all who believe in Him. Fifty days later the Holy Spirit shows up on the scene. Believers are empowered and commissioned to go unto the world to preach the gospel and make disciples, to display God's perfect will, to bring heaven down, to display how powerful it is to be one with God, to shape and influence culture, to heal the sick, to love everyone, to be selfless, to chase their God given dreams, to live with purpose, to model how to do business the Kingdom way, to model how to lead families, communities, and companies, to model how we should treat each other, to model Christ exalting marriages, to model creativity the Kingdom way, to be the light and the salt of the world. Ultimately becoming like Christ. Illuminating this world with God's light.

To claim this freedom purchased at the cross, we must believe in Christ. When you believe in Christ, your-self dies with Him and you rise up a new man or woman, you become a new creation. Why die to self? Because it is the sinful nature we are born in; self is the part of humans that listens to satan. It's the part of humans satan has mastered to manipulate.

This sounds like the end of the story, right? Die to self and rise up with Jesus and boom, you live in the glorious new reality for all believers, right? I mean, the enemy's got nothing on you right? The truth is that if we are honest, this is not a reality for most of us. Most of us are still haunted by the ghosts of our former selves.

The Word of God says: "the devil prowls around like a roaring lion looking for someone to devour" (1 Peter 5:8, NIV). But we all know no one is stupid enough to throw himself or herself to an angry roaring lion, unless you're Benaiah, who was courageous, and a little crazy. Let's take a moment to look at this imagery of a roaring lion and expand the idea. The angry roaring lion won't draw you to himself by roaring; he knows it's not going to work. He knows that human instinct is to run when you hear a roar of a lion or any dangerous creature. Being a trickster, he uses a trick to manipulate you. He uses the ghost of your-former-self to draw you out. The former you. The you that died with Christ. He knows that you've lived all your life with it. It was who you were from birth, you are accustomed to it, and you are comfortable with it. Listening to it is listening to your own voice. It's like looking in the mirror. The ideas, the language, the tone, the jokes, the metaphors, the reactions, and the sympathy, are all you. So it feels safe. He slowly gets your attention. The moment you engage, you are prone to lethal danger. Because you don't see the devil in this conversation, you see and hear your-self. You are engaging in a conversation with the father of deceit and lies, whose expertise is to get you lost, but you're thinking that you are talking to yourself.

Just like that, many have delivered themselves to the yoke of the deceiver. This is level one.

His roar is louder the darker it gets. This is level two. The manipulation is severe the more confusing it gets. The lies are sicker the more painful it gets. He is the master deceiver. He will use the darkest hour to his advantage. He will pose a roar in the middle of the path God has set before you. A roar that suggests you will be devoured if you take any further steps. Struck with fear, you stop moving. He then uses your dead self to talk you out of your calling, dream, and breakthrough. Everything makes sense at this point. There is a roar in the middle of the path. This roar could be the researched facts that people no longer buy music, especially gospel records, so stepping out to make music for Christ will lead to starvation. It could simply be that thriving in business will require corruption and you're a Christian, so you won't thrive without corruption, quit. It could be statistics of people who have failed at what you are being called to. It could be people who tell you that you won't succeed at what you are called to do. The roar is loud. God is quiet. Your logic, which is really the enemy talking, seems to make sense. Now you have a decision to make. To call him out and say, "Get behind me satan" and ignore his roar and press on because the presence of the Lord is with you, the Lion of Judah is with you, a Lion who devoured satan at the cross. Or will you heed to the lies of the shortsighted manipulative and doomed satan?

The devil will use dark times to deceive you and talk you out of your destiny, even your ultimate destiny, becoming like Christ Jesus, our Lord. I don't know if you are getting this, I really hope you get it. The voice that's been telling you...

You are a failure and loser

You don't have it in you

You are not qualified

You're making a fool of yourself

You will never overcome this

You will never heal

You are cursed

It's too late for you, the ship has sailed

Why don't you try something else?

God won't use you, why would He?

What makes you think you'll be the first one to do this?

You'll be a laughing stock so walk away now!

All this time you're thinking these are your sound, smart, calculated and wise ideas. While all along you've been snared into a conversation with the devil. He's been whispering into your mind using your own voice. Manipulating the process God is taking you to purify you into Christlikeness. Stealing your joy, your peace, your freedom, and your fearless nature. Stealing the life and future God has for you, and just like that, men and women give up their freedom that entail living out the glorious life Jesus died so we can have. But no more, I say no more, I challenge you to say no more. NO MORE!!! It's time to wake up and rise two levels up.

The Word of God says, "Submit yourself to God, resist the devil and he will flee" (James 4:7, NIV). The life of the called, the dreamers, the ones becoming like Christ can be a painful life, a life of suffering. But there's great joy in the midst of this suffering. It's easy to miss out on the joy and focus on the suffering. Sometimes there aren't answers as to why things happen to us. Sometimes no one can understand the pain you are going through. Sometimes no one can comfort you. But in the midst of all of this, there's great joy to be found in the presence of the Lord.

12

Functioning perspective

I never cease to be amazed by the genius of God in creation. He placed in each one of us such complex and beautiful abilities to decipher life. Perspective is one of those gifts. Perspective is such an individualistic quality that two people can be looking at the same thing but see two completely different things. The freedom of perspective granted to us by God is a pure gift. It attests to the gift of free will bestowed on us. God doesn't force Himself unto anyone. He loves to be found.

Perspective is one of the major gifts God has graced us with to fully equip us in the ability to find and locate Him and His will in every situation. He gave us the freedom of perspective in the hopes that we will find Him and see His working hand in every situation. God likes to be found so much that He rewards those who find Him. A good example is the twelve spies sent to Canaan to investigate the land (Numbers 13). Upon their return, ten of them hadn't seen God, they saw giants and walls. But Joshua and Caleb saw God and His powerful hand at work. Both twelve were granted the same gift of perspective and the freedom to choose what to perceive, but only two saw God, meeting God's desire to be found. Those two are the only ones who entered the Promised Land. Perspective is a gift from God; the underlying purpose of perspective is finding God in all that we perceive. In finding God, we attest to His presence, thus glorifying His nature and person. Ultimately, perspective is a gift that is meant to act as a means to glorify God.

When you don't know the purpose of something, you abuse it. We live our lives abusing the gift of perspective because we don't even know its purpose. The purpose is to glorify the Lord by locating Him and His will in every situation and circumstance. Does your perspective about everything glorify God? Perspective is not designed to serve our intellectual needs and curiosities. It is meant to serve God. It is your job to find God in how you perceive things. Majority of us jump ship when things go from bad to worse because our perspective fails to locate God in the situation. What a lie. The more difficult the situation, the harder you look for God in that situation. The purpose of perspective is to locate God in every situation and season in your life. The failure to locate God in a situation or season is basically putting our perspective into dysfunction mode.

Use the gift of perspective to locate God in the process you are in. When things go from bad to worse, use your perspective to locate God and stop using your perspective to locate a way out. Many of us have given up on our dreams, our breakthroughs, and our callings, because we were quicker to locate a way out than to locate God and His will.

Jesus illustrates perspective very well in the gospel of Luke.

"No one, when he has lit a lamp, puts it in a secret place or under a basket, but on a lampstand, that those who come in may see the light. The lamp of the body is the eye. Therefore, when your eye is good, your whole body also is full of light. But when your eye is bad, your body also is full of darkness" (Luke 11:33-36).

Let me bring this into context. Jesus had been doing a lot of amazing and out of this world things all over Israel. The blind received sight, the deaf heard again, the lame started walking, the dead came back to life and food was miraculously multiplied. His wisdom was way above the wisdom of Solomon. All signs pointed to Jesus being the promised Messiah. But the people didn't see it. In fact, they accused him of using Beelzebub juju power to cast out demons. I mean, who accuses Jesus of getting His power from some Kalumanzila jungle juju? They put Jesus on the stand. They wanted a sign. All the while many prophecies about Him were at their disposal in the scriptures. John the Baptist cosigned Jesus; he said Jesus is the Guy they have been waiting for. But these guys didn't budge. They didn't bother locating and finding God and His Word concerning Jesus. While God did the biggest cosign on the day Jesus was baptized for the people to hear, their perspective was so dysfunctional that instead of locating God and His Word, they were seeking a sign, yet they were completely blind to all the signs already in front of them, and the scriptures. Jesus calls them an evil generation. A generation that fails to locate God, His Word and His will; a generation whose perspective is perverted. He went on to say that as a matter of fact, the people of Nineveh will condemn it because those guys repented after hearing sermons from a guy who got swallowed by a big fish. His name is Jonah. The people of Nineveh were able to locate God and see His holiness and it exposed their sins, they had to repent and they did. But the generation of Jesus had such a dysfunctional perspective they didn't see the Messiah. Now that we are on the same page, no pun intended, let's continue.

The scripture (Luke 11:33-36) is such a powerful illustration of perspective. The Lord is pointing out that their problem is their dysfunctional perspective, that's why they don't even see that He is the promised Messiah. The

Lord first talks about a lamp and He identifies its core function-providing light. That light graces people the ability to see things and locate things. Lighting a lamp and hiding it defeats the purpose. In fact, He says no one does this. It's almost like He is saying, "It is nothing short of ridiculous to light a lamp and then hide it." He then goes on to say the lamp of the body is the eye, therefore, when your eye is good your whole body also is full of light. He is saying when you're perspective is functioning in its original purpose of locating God, your whole life will have a sense of a clear direction. When your perspective can locate God, then no situation in life will draw you away from His will. Jesus then wraps it up with a statement that describes the lives most of us live. He says "but when your eye is bad, your body also is full of darkness." When your perspective fails to locate God, then your whole life is doomed. He uses the word darkness for a purpose, because when we are in a dark place the first instinct is to locate a way out. This is a tragic life. Many of us have been so overwhelmed by the darkness around us that we zealously locate a way out. Jesus compares us to the insane people who light a lamp and hide it. When things go from bad to worse in the process, without putting our perspective into its rightful function of locating God, we will always find ourselves locating a way out. Because all we can see is darkness. Looking for a way out instead of locating the Light of the world, Christ Jesus.

In the gospel of John chapter 11, we read the story of one of Jesus's good friends, a guy named Lazarus. Lazarus was very sick and about to die, and his sisters Martha and Mary decide to make a very wise decision of sending word to Jesus, letting Him know that His boy Lazarus is very sick. Jesus receives this news and then He decides to stay two more days where He is. The Bible doesn't say how long Jesus took before going to Bethany. The only information we have is that by the time Jesus was there, Lazarus was dead for four days. So it's possible that Jesus might have taken a whole week before finally going to Bethany. This story is a perfect illustration of a functioning perspective. If you look on the surface, it looks like Jesus doesn't really care about Lazarus. I mean, if He did then He would've dropped everything and journeyed to Bethany. Instead, He does a despicable thing by taking His time and leaving Lazarus to die. Leaving his friends Martha and Mary under the torment and agony of watching their brother die. This is how the situation looks like on the surface. Jesus was the breakthrough Martha and Mary were waiting for but Jesus fell through. Lazarus died, all hope was gone, and all they could see was darkness. They absolutely failed to locate God in their situation. They had a dysfunctional perspective. Four days into the death of Lazarus, Jesus shows up. What Martha and Mary thought was a missed opportunity for healing, turns into an opportunity for resurrection. Jesus had a functioning perspective. He located God in the situation. When others saw death, He saw life. He knew that the power for resurrection stems from God.

Most of the time what stumbles us is our own presumed ways out of situations and challenges. We sit and we analyze. We come to a conclusion that God, if you do this and that, this will be the result that's best for me. "Jesus if you would've come earlier Lazarus would still be alive" (John 11:21, my paraphrase) and all Jesus is telling you is, "trust in Me, abide in Me, locate Me in your situation. I know the plans and thoughts I have for you, let Me deal with the details, and you concern yourself with locating Me and seeking Me with all you have." Jesus says in verse 25, "I am the resurrection and life. He who believes in Me, though he may die he shall live. And whoever lives and believes in Me shall never die" (John 11:25).

Having a functioning perspective is a rare quality in our world today. When you apply your faith, people will often think you're delusional and crazy. They will brand you as unrealistic because your perspective is not limited by what is seen with the naked eye. Your perspective sees endless possibilities for God to be glorified in every situation.

The functioning perspective Jesus talked about lies in God. It doesn't lie in your intellect and resources, it lies in God. It doesn't lie in you knowing who you are, but in knowing who God is. A functioning perspective sees every impossible situation as an opportunity to invite God to fix it, to give life, to transform, to resurrect, to open doors and to strengthen.

Having a functioning perspective is seeing life while others see death because you know the Lord you serve is the resurrection and life. It is seeing a possibility while others see obstacles because the Lord you serve makes a way where there's no way. A functioning perspective knows who God is; that God is all-powerful, all knowing, all good, all able and all sovereign. So while others see darkness, you see light. When others see things falling apart, you see Him putting together a better thing. When others see the impossible, you see an opportunity for God to be glorified.

When you start to look at every tough and impossible situation in your process as an opportunity to locate God and invite Him in so He can be glorified, you will experience great things.

As a believer of Christ Jesus, your perspective is the most functional in this world. Your perspective can locate the Life Giver, Miracle worker, Most Holy Problem Solver in the entire universe. Your perspective lives with the utmost assurance because the God you serve has said, "Surely, as I have thought, so it shall come to pass, And as I have purposed, so it shall stand" (Isaiah 14:24). And you know that He also said "For I know the thoughts that I think toward you, says the LORD, thoughts of peace and not of evil, to give you a future and a hope" (Jeremiah 29:11). As if this is not enough, His Word says, "All things work together for good to those who love God, to those who are called according to His purpose" (Romans 8:28). As a believer of Christ this is your reality. But you have to locate God in your process. When things go from bad to worse, His Word still stands. What He has purposed shall stand and what He has thought shall come to pass. This is your reality. This is the truth. But you have to locate God. He is right there with you, working the worst that you think is happening for your good. The problem is that when things go from good to worse or bad to worst, most us are quick to locate a way out. Our perspectives have been so perverted that we don't even see the need to locate God. And we shut down any prompting the Holy Spirit will give us. Many dreams have died this way. Many breakthroughs have fallen through this way. Many relationships and marriages have died this way. And many have forfeited God's will for their lives this very same way. No more! You need to take control over the gift of perspective God has given you. Don't allow the enemy to pervert it. Use it to locate God in your process. God will not call you just to show you a way out. God will not give you a dream just for you to give up on it. When the going gets tough, the Christ-like get going.

Often in the process we drown ourselves in the word "reality." We tell ourselves, "Let's get real now." We have elevated realism to a point of relegating God. Anything that is not conceivable with our minds is optimistic and not real, thus inadmissible. When good becomes bad then God is not in it. When the possible becomes impossible then it's a sign to check out. When the joyful becomes painful then it's our cue to leave. But let me paint a picture for you. If Jesus were as we call it, "being real," Lazarus would've stayed dead. If David was keeping it real, he would've never faced Goliath. If Joshua and Caleb were realists, they wouldn't have seen the Promised Land. If Noah were a realist like the rest of the people in his time, he wouldn't have spent 120 years building an Ark in a dessert land. You want to keep it real? Locate God in every step of your process and see how your reality becomes unrealistic to this world. When your perspective is functional, the day things go from bad to worse and the world tells you, "hey get real!" remind them that your reality is unrealistic to their world.

13

The great encouragement

Another person whose situation went from bad to worse is Apostle Paul. He was whipped, stoned, beaten and imprisoned. Paul pretty much spent most of his life on the worse-end rather than the good or even the bad. In the book of Philippians, we find Paul near the end of his life, in a Roman prison for preaching the gospel. He is supposed to be taking the gospel to the world and preaching to kings and here he is, stuck in this lonely hell. Talk about a discouraging situation. But in this inhuman condition, Paul reveals something beautiful. But before he reveals it, he talks a big game about how the Philippi Christians should follow his example. They should live their lives the way he lives his. This alone reveals that Paul was not grumpy when things went from good to worse. He then tells them to manage their thoughts; whatever is good, noble, praise worthy, lovely, pure and anything with virtue they should meditate on such things. Biblical meditating is muttering or simply talking to thyself. Paul is telling them, you need to learn to encourage yourself. Look for anything good, noble, praise worthy, lovely, pure and anything with virtue you can find to encourage yourself. Please note, that I am talking about human encouragement. You will be in situations and seasons where only you can encourage yourself, so learn to do so. But this is not Paul's homerun as far as the great encouragement is concerned. Paul is just warming up. Because encouraging yourself can only take you so far. There are things that require divine intervention to walk through. He says, "For I have learned to be content whatever the circumstances. I know what it is to be in need, and I know what it is to have plenty. I have learned the secret of being content in any and every situation, whether well fed or hungry, whether living in plenty or in want. I can do all this through Him who gives me strength" (Philippians 4:11-13, NIV).

Imagine being in the Philippi church when this letter first reached you. And the pastor reads this letter to you for the first time, and you hear the words, "I have learned the secret of being content in any and every situation" and your excitement builds up because you think Paul is about to reveal some aerodynamic secrets. Then Paul says, "I can do all things through Christ who gives me strength" (Philippians 4:13).

You go,

"Wait a minute, what? I thought you were about to reveal how I can get out of this misery and you're saying that I have to walk through it? If we can do all things, then we should be able to get wings to fly us out of tough situations, I like this version of content, Paul!"

Paul's secret for being content in any and every situation echoes a lot of pain. It shuts down our dreams of escape. It reveals that contentment requires walking through things. But the great encouragement is that Christ will give you strength to walk through it. And while you're walking through it, you need to learn to encourage yourself.

You are able to walk through your darkest hour because Christ gives you strength to walk through it. You can walk through loss, death, confusion, bankruptcy, rejection, failure, persecution, pain and lack because Christ gives you strength to walk through it. When things go from bad to worse in your process, Jesus will not give you a parachute to jump off the plane, He will give you strength to go through it. He will give you strength to be content while going through it. There isn't a circumstance or situation that Christ will fail to give you strength to walk through it. There isn't a circumstance or situation that Christ will fail to consume you to a point where you become content while walking through it. The great encouragement is not that your darkest hour will pass too quickly or that you will be exempted. The great encouragemnet is that Christ will give you strength to walk through it. Glory to the risen King. But I don't think we should end here, I think there's a great secret within Paul's secret.

SATAN'S NUCLEAR

Two men, Adam and Jesus, carried the destiny of all of mankind. Adam failed. Jesus was victorious. But since these two men carried the entire destiny of mankind, it's worth our while to study the nature of the temptations the enemy shoved their way. Because the enemy knew that if he defeats these two guys, then he's defeated all of mankind. And in studying the nature of these temptations we will uncover the killers of destinies. Let's start with Adam.

Who He says He is

Now the serpent was more crafty than any other beast of the field that the Lord God had made. He said to the woman, "Did God actually say, 'You shall not eat of any tree in the garden'?" And the woman said to the serpent, "We may eat of the fruit of the trees in the garden, but God said, 'You shall not eat of the fruit of the tree that is in the midst of the garden, neither shall you touch it, lest you die'" But the serpent said to the woman, "*You will not surely die. For God knows that when you eat of it your eyes will be opened, and you will be like God, knowing good and evil*" (Genesis 3:1-5, ESV).

Satan's first nuclear weapon is destroying your view of who God is. The narrative of the fall starts halfway through, the question the serpent asks suggests that there was a prior conversation, when was this conversation had? We don't know, but it's important to note this because his question suggests that Eve had been resisting the temptation. Satan says, "Did God actually say, 'You shall not eat of any tree in the garden'?" This question is proof that there was a conversation before this sentence and Eve had resisted the temptation and shut down his lies. So satan changes gear, and goes into unleashing his nuclear attack. He tells the woman, "You will not surely die. For God knows that when you eat of it your eyes will be opened, and you will be like God, knowing good and evil." This response is aimed at destroying the character of God, and now Eve is questioning God and His Word, she is probably wondering that God is surely holding them back from reaching their full potential by putting this rule. She no longer believes that God has her best interest at heart. What does she do? She eats and gives the fruit to Adam, sin, death and chaos enters the world, and every human being is doomed. Satan wins, Adam loses.

Satan destroys Eve's faith that believes God is, who He says He is. This is one of his two major weapons. When satan wants to destroy you and your destiny, he works at destroying your view of God, your faith. When you have the wrong view of who God is and who He says He is, you are in a lot of trouble. Is your faith intact? Does God's own Word support your view of who He is? This is paramount.

Who He say you are

And the tempter came and said to him, "*If you are the Son of God*, command these stones to become loaves of bread." But He answered, "it is written, "'Man shall not live by bread alone, but by every Word that comes from the mouth of God.'" Then the devil took him to the holy city and set him on the pinnacle of the temple and said to him, "*If you are the Son of God*, throw yourself down, for it is written, "'He will command his angels concerning you,' and "'On their hands they will bear you up, lest you strike your foot against a stone.'" Jesus said to him, "Again it is written, 'You shall not put the Lord your God to the test.'" Again, the devil took Him to a very high mountain and showed Him all the kingdoms of the world and their glory. And he said to Him, "All these I will give you, if you will fall down and worship me." Then Jesus said to him, "Be gone, satan! For it is written, "'You shall worship the Lord your God and him only shall you serve'" (Matthew 4:3-10, ESV).

Jesus was the second Man on whom the destiny of mankind rested upon. For thousands of years mankind was suffering because of Adam's sin and Jesus was the Person who was going to change all of this, but before this, He needs to be tempted. So the Spirit leads Him to the wilderness to be tempted. And the enemy gets another shot at destroying the destiny of mankind. But he knows a little something about Jesus, so his approach changes a little bit. With Jesus, he uses his second most powerful nuclear weapon. Why the second and not the first? I think it's probably because he knew that there was no way he could possibly convince Jesus that the Father wasn't who He says He is. At least not in an obvious way. So he goes for his second best weapon, which is the same as first, only craftier, destroying who God says you are.

The prelude to this time of temptation in the wilderness is the baptism of Jesus. During which God explicitly said, "This is my beloved Son, in whom I am well pleased." Key words here being, "beloved Son" not just "Son." "Beloved Son" because there are many sons of God, some of which fell from heaven and were the agents of serious abominations during the times of Noah (Genesis 6:1-4), but Jesus is the beloved Son of God. The blissful moment of baptism was over, Jesus is now in the wilderness, no food, no water, wild animals around, then the devil takes his shot at destroying the destiny of mankind.

He asks Jesus three questions, but the first two are similar. In the first two questions, he starts off by saying, "If you are the Son of God..." Wait a minute, Jesus was not just a Son of God, He is the beloved Son of God. You may think this omission is not a big deal, but this omission changes the entire identity of Christ. Because if this word beloved wasn't a big deal God wouldn't have said it, because God doesn't waste His Words. So the omission was meant to lead Christ to question His own identity. But Jesus was many steps ahead of satan. He countered the argument of satan by ignoring the omission and focusing on shutting down his manipulative exegesis by quoting another part of the Word of God. Because while the scripture the enemy quoted is true, it was not the full truth. The enemy took it out of context and omitted parts that would destroy his agenda. You can see that while the devil was focused on destroying who God says Jesus is, Jesus was focused on holding on to the right view of who God is. Satan tried this trick twice and it failed, and his last attempt was so weak that Jesus kicked him out. If Jesus had focused on the identity crisis suggested by the omission, He probably would've missed out on how wrong the enemy was in quoting Psalm 91.

The enemy's second most powerful weapon is destroying what God says about you. In the process, the enemy will work his very best to destroy and pervert what God says about Himself and what He says about you. Because these two lies will kill your destiny. Is your view of who God says He is right? Is your view of who God says you are right?

How does this relate to Paul? Let's go back to the scripture, Paul says, "I can do all things through Him who gives me strength." Note that the secret within the secret here is that, Paul had the right view of what God says about Himself. God has made many promises in His Word, but Paul didn't have the New Testament scripture at his time, the available scripture at the time was the Old Testament scripture. And in that, among many things God had said, He said, "Fear not, for I am with you; be not dismayed, for I am your God; I will strengthen you, I will help you, I will uphold you with my righteous right hand" (Isaiah 41:10). And Paul believed this promise with all of his heart. He believed that God will strengthen him; He believed that God was his source of strength regardless of the situation. But Paul also had the right view of what God said about him, because Holy Scriptures also said, "but those who wait on the Lord shall renew their strength; they shall mount up with wings like eagles; they shall run and not be weary; they shall walk and not faint" (Isaiah 40:31). God had said that those who have placed their hope in Him will not be weary, they will walk and not faint, no circumstance will overcome them. And Paul believed this with every inch of his being. The secret of Paul hung on these two things. Having the right view of who God says He is. And having the right view of who God says you are. This is the great encouragement. Do you know what God says about Himself? Do you know the character of God? Do you know Him personally? Do you know what God says about you? When things go from good to worse in the process, the great encouragement rests in these two things.

the internship for your destiny the internship for your destiny **the internship for your destiny** the internship for your destiny **the internship for your destiny** the internship for your destiny **the internship for your destiny** the internship for your destiny **the internship for your destiny** the internship for your destiny **the internship for your destiny** the internship for your destiny **the internship for your destiny** the internship for y

When a full picture God directs your big picture story

14

The full picture God

There's a bigger picture to your life, a picture that you will never live to fully grasp. It transcends generations. It goes to ten generations after you and beyond. This is how your life works. It's not just you, there's a bigger picture to who you are, your story and your impact, good or bad. So, like how any good story needs a narrator or a director to lead it to its rightful climax. Your story also needs someone who will lead it to its rightful climax. The director you choose is the most important decision you will make.

So in search for a perfect director for your story we encounter God. Only to realize He is the One pursuing you, persuading you to choose Him and allow Him to be the director of your story. Now, let's look at the profile of this Director. First, He is Omniscient, which means He knows everything. He knows the end before the beginning, and nothing that has happened or will happen takes Him by surprise. He is aware of everything that will ever happen for eternity.

Second, He is Omnipotent, which means He is all-powerful. He can make things happen for you. He can move mountains for you. Nothing is impossible to Him. Thirdly, He is Omnipresent, which means He is always present. He is present everywhere, all the time. He is present in your future. He is present in the minds of your enemies. He is present in the minds of those who will offer you opportunities. He is present in the storms you will face. He is present in the adversaries that will come your way years to come. He is always present, to both the antagonist and the protagonist. He is also good, there's no evil in Him, there's no sin in Him and all that He does is good.

He is love; everything He does is from the place of love. Love is not something He wants to attain, He is the actual Love. He is faithful; this means He is a God of His Word. What He says He will surely do. What He has purposed will surely come to pass. Everything will pass but His Word shall stand.

And I will like to close with this nature of His. He is perfect. This means He will never change or grow or stumble upon something new. Who He is, is exactly who He has always been and who He will always be. Forever.

These are the only truths we need as a basis to trust God. This is the nature and character you need the director of your life and destiny to have. God, the one who desires to direct your big picture story. He is all knowing, which means He sees the full picture. He is a full picture God. He exists outside of time. Full picture is His perspective. Who is better to direct your story than He? You're a big picture story. He is a full picture God. Perfect match. But for there to be harmony, for God to be able to do what His does best, there has to be trust. He needs you to trust Him with all your heart. There can't be doubt in this relationship. Doubt is a killer in this relationship. It won't jeopardize God. It's going to jeopardize you and your story. That's why trust is very important in this relationship. Speaking of trust. This is such an interesting word. Trust as used in Proverbs 3:5 is the word baw-takh' which means to hie for refuge; figuratively, to trust, be confident or sure—be bold (confident, secure, sure). This is trust. So in context, trust is to be confident in who God is. Rushing to Him for refuge. To be utterly confident of who He is and who He says you are.

Trust in relationship with God is believing in Him even when it doesn't make sense to us. It's surrendering our confusion to His understanding. Using His word and direction to make decisions, and not our confusion and lack of understanding. But sometimes we dumb down trust to believing someone on the merit of what we understand with our feeble minds. We treat God like the next guy. Until it makes sense to our feeble minds then it's inadmissible. We have sized God down to our tiny brains. If the facts don't make sense then we can't bank our lives on it. Basically saying He can't be trusted to direct our stories.

But let's be real, who needs to trust God when everything "makes sense?" Who needs trust when everything is laid out before you? There's no room for trust if every decision is based on the presentation of facts. We see this in court. The judge doesn't make final judgments based on trust but based on facts presented, facts that opposing sides will question for verification. Facts you take an oath to present. Facts that will be questioned when new evidence surfaces. This is not trust. This is factual belief. But trust is deeper than this. Trust is taking God at His Word even when things don't make sense. This is why God is the most trustworthy above everyone. He has a track record that shows He is never wrong. In fact, He is all knowing, how can He be wrong?

Yet we put God on trial with the enemy as our sidekick attorney and our minds as both the jury and the judge. This is our version of trust. We treat God like He is a dodgy Person. You know, the one who acts as if He's got you but you always wonder, are you really for me?

We can donate all our brains to make one giant brain, I mean everyone who ever lived, plus angels and the ones who never get tired of saying Holy! Holy! Holy! at His throne and still His foolishness will outsmart us (1 Corinthians 1:25, NIV). Yet we still gather enough courage to put Him on the stand. Why don't we just learn from Job who tried this and received a divine reality check?

Job was questioning God when his life didn't make sense, or rather let's just say it was going from bad to worse. God shut him up. He asked him some pretty basic questions. He said, okay Job, since you are so smart, please tell me "Where were you when I laid the foundations of the earth? Have you commanded the morning since your days began, and cause the dawn to know its place? Can you send out lightning, that they may go, And say to you, 'Here we are?' Who provides food for the raven, when its young ones cry to God, and wander about for the lack of food?" (Job 38). God sure knows how to set the record straight and send crazy talk back where it belongs.

Don't get me wrong. I am not saying it's wrong to ask God questions, it is good to ask Him questions. After all, He wants a relationship. But there is a difference between asking God questions and questioning God. When you ask God questions it's because you want to know some things that you don't know but your view of God is still right. But when you question God it's because you doubt Him and His character. Abraham asked God many questions when God was about to destroy Sodom. God answered all his questions. Abraham asked because he wanted to know, he didn't question the character of God. You can read this story in Genesis 18:16-33.

But most of us have a blind eye on this and we don't even want to admit that our trust has been perverted. So even though God speaks for Himself, I want to make a case with you using His Word. I hope at the end of this act you will trust God wholeheartedly and submit your process to Him. Now I want to start this act by going into a time machine and go all the way back to the years 1013 BC - 970 BC in the time of a boy named David Jesse. I will use his life as a backdrop to show you how God uses the process to prepare you for your destiny. I hope at the end of this act you will desire to be faithful in your process more than you desire to reach your destination. I hope at the end of this act you will see how far your story goes and the generations that will be touched by your life. My hope is that this act will lead you into complete submission to the Lord Christ Jesus if you are still unconvinced up to this point.

Character - based destiny

Every destiny has a character requirement. The requirement is different based on your destiny. Of cause there are the common denominators that we all need, but each destiny requires certain character from you. If you are called to be a teacher, the character requirement of your destiny will be different from someone who is called to be a president or a missionary in Pakistan. The destiny God created you for determines the character requirement to grow into. Your character requirement is what determines the process where God develops your character.

Israel was God's chosen nation. God loved this nation very deeply. He had been their king for a long time. The people wanted to have a human king. God gave them Saul, but not before He warned them of what to expect. With the rise and fall of Saul, a royal office was officially established. But God chose for Himself a man from the house of Judah. David Jesse was called to be the king over Israel. God chose him to reign over His people. David's destiny was the throne of Israel. This destiny required certain character from David. This requirement is what determined David's process. So lets' take a look at some of the character requirements that his destiny required. We will also see how God used the process to develop these virtues.

EXALTING GOD

God wanted a king that would exalt Him above everything and everyone. This was one of the core characters required. Israel was a nation surrounded by pagan nations and God wanted to establish His righteous rule through Israel. This is only possible when the ruler of the place exalts God to His rightful place. David needed to be this kind of person.

David was considered the least in his own family. His father and brothers despised him. He spent most of his time alone tending sheep in the forest. This is where he developed a deeper relationship with the Lord. In his popular psalm he says 'The Lord is my shepherd I lack nothing" (Psalm 23:1, NIV). He lived a life where those who were supposed to believe in him didn't so David turned to God. God became everything for David. God was number one. God was David's Father. He became everything David ever needed. David learned to exalt God through obscurity and rejection.

God kept putting David in positions where this virtue was perfected.

Saul was hunting David with the intention of killing him, David runs and hides in a cave. He was lonely and confused at this point in his life. Wondering what happened, because a short while ago he was considered a national hero and women sang songs about him. Yet he finds himself alone in a cave, like prey hiding from a predator. It's in this cave that David wrote psalm 142. Parts of the psalm say, "Look on my right hand and see, For there is no one who acknowledges me; Refuge has failed me; No one cares for my soul" (v. 4). But it was in these moments that David learned to exalt God and depend on Him and not his "social status" or friends in the "higher places" David went on to say "I cried out to You, O Lord: I said, "You are my refuge, My portion in the land of the living" (v. 5).

Through different circumstances, David learnt to exalt God above all else. He needed to learn this because his destiny required it. Exalting God was David's greatest asset. God used obscurity and rejection to create this in David.

BRAVERY

David's destiny required bravery. A king who will see God's might above his own strength. God saw all the battles Israel would face, so bravery was key for the king.

God went on to use the wilderness to develop this character in David. David nurtured his bravery by killing bears and lions. He achieved this in his teenage years. This bravery got him ready to face Goliath, and when the opportunity to face Goliath came, he killed him with one shot. The entire Israel army, full of trained and skilled soldiers, was afraid because they saw their strength against Goliath's. But David saw God's strength versus Goliath's. Bravery in the dictionary of God is seeing His power above your own strength. God used the tending sheep days to train David in the art of sling shooting and battle strategy but above all He trained David to see the Lord's strength and not his own.

David was not wasting time tending sheep in the wilderness. He was in God's military academy. It was his boot camp where God was developing the bravery inside of David. Bravery required by his destiny. The wilderness was essential for David. The battles in his destiny depended on it.

GOD FEARING

If a king was going to lead God's people, he had to fear the Lord. David was put in many situations where he had to sharpen his fear of the Lord. When Saul was hunting David to kill him, David had plenty of opportunity to kill Saul but refused because he feared the Lord. In fact, David had a group of fugitive warriors that were hiding with him; a group of warriors that sacrificed their lives and freedom to serve David. They believed in David, the choice that put them on Saul's most wanted list, the penalty of which was death. So David didn't have the luxury to disappoint these guys. Yet when an opportunity to kill Saul came, David refused, even after being urged by his fugitive warriors. He feared God and not men. He had spent most of his life alone and learned to exalt God and fear Him. He didn't care what others felt. His desire was to please God. God knew that David's future consisted of making tough decisions against what others think in obedience to where He is leading him. So his fear of God had to be sharpened and his fear of men had to die.

COMPASSION AND CARE FOR THOSE YOU ARE RESPONSIBLE FOR

God wanted a leader who will be compassionate, a leader who will care for His people. One who would look after the nation as he would his own children. David was trained to care for those he looks after. God used the wilderness to develop in David a tender heart towards those he cares for. We see this when David goes the extra mile to protect his flock of sheep. He kills a lion and a bear that try to kill his sheep. He risked his life for the sake of sheep. This was the character God wanted for the king over his people, a king who would go to the ends of the earth to protect His people.

When David was put in charge of playing the stress freeing music in the royal palace, he cared for his king. The Bible tells us that David was consistent in his responsibility to soothe the king when he was distressed. David displayed care in the most macho ways and in the most tender ways. This was the kind of king God wanted for Israel. He used different seasons and places to develop this in David.

CRISIS MANAGEMENT

God wanted a king who would know how to manage crisis. The royal office required this character trait. The king would face many trials and needed to be a good crisis manager. God put David in many crisis situations so he can learn how to manage them. In 1 Samuel 23:1-5 David the fugitive gets the information that the Philistines are fighting against Keilah and they are stealing their food reserve. As much as he hated the Philistines, his first action was to inquire from God, and God said "Go and attack the Philistines, and save Keilah" (1 Samuel 23:2). When he told his men that it's time to go fight the Philistines, they weren't on board with his plan. They believed it to be a suicide mission. And they were right because Keilah was a gated city, only one way to go in and come out. Going in will be delivering themselves to Saul in a silver platter. David found himself caught in the crossroads; he can't go to fight alone, but at the same time, God gave him the go-ahead. In the heat of the crisis, David decides to go back to God and inquire again, to which God says, "Arise, go down to Keilah. For I will deliver the Philistines into your hand" (1 Samuel 23:4).

We see this again in 1 Samuel 30:1-8, where David returns to Ziklag after being dismissed from service by Achish the prince of Gath. Ziklag was David's home at this point in his life, it was also the home of his men and their families, both wives and children. David and his men come home and find ruins left by the attack from the Amalekites, and all their wives and children taken captive. David is extremely distressed, and weeps until he is out of tears. The people of Ziklag are frustrated and in pain so they plan to take it out on David by stoning him. After all, David was supposed to be their protector and he wasn't there to protect them. In the heat of this crisis, people want to stone David. His wives are taken captive, the families of his loyal men are taken captive, and their properties are stolen. The Bible says David strengthened himself in the Lord. David then proceeds with his usual crisis management routine. He goes and inquiries from God what to do, and God says, "Pursue, for you shall surely overtake them and without fail recover all" (1 Samuel 30:8).

David's calling required him to be a man who knows how to manage crisis. Beginning with seeking counsel from God in every crisis before taking any further steps. God took him through a process to prepare him and train him in this trait. So all the trials he faced where he had to manage a crisis was actually the internship for his destiny.

DESIRE TO GLORIFY GOD

God wanted a king with a deep desire to glorify Him. He wanted someone who will do what it takes to glorify the Lord. David was this kind of guy. He was all about glorifying the Lord. In his process, he was trained to do what it takes to make sure God is glorified. We see this put into action in the first book of Samuel: "Then David said to the Philistine, "You come to me with a sword, with a spear, and with a javelin. But I come to you in the name of the Lord of hosts, the God of the armies of Israel, whom you have defied. This day the Lord will deliver you into my hand, and I will strike you and take your head from you. And this day I will give the carcasses of the camp of the Philistines to the birds of the air and the wild beasts of the earth, that all the earth may know that there is a God in Israel. Then all this assembly shall know that the Lord does not save with sword and spear; for the battle is the Lord's, and He will give you into our hands" (1 Samuel 17:45-47). David couldn't stand there and listen to Goliath mock God's chosen nation, because mocking Israel was mocking God, and this kind of thing didn't fly with David. David desired to glorify God, and this was his opportunity to show how far he will go to make sure God gets the glory. David risked his life to make sure the world knows who God is and how He delivers His people from deathly odds. This is the kind of king God wanted to reign over His people.

TRUST IN GOD

The destiny of David required him to build complete trust in God. A king immersed with faith in the Lord. One who wouldn't use common sense over faith. God wanted a king who would take Him at His Word. He took David through different seasons and tribulations to test and purify his faith. David's faith was tested in the wilderness killing lions and bears. His faith was again tested in the valley of Elah when he faced Goliath. His faith was tested when Saul wanted to kill him, it was also tested when he had chances to avenge Saul. But David trusted God to put him on the throne in His own time and His own way. Through all these dire moments, David's faith was purified. David needed complete trust in God if he was going to rule over His people. As king, he would face many adversaries and without trusting in the Lord, he would fail.

JUST

God wanted a king who loved justice, a king who would exercise justice over His people. The Lord wanted a king who would not oppress those he has power over. God gave David plenty of opportunities to nurture this fruit. We see this in 1 Samuel 30:21-23. After God gave him a go-ahead to pursue, attack and recover everything from the Amalekites, two hundred of David's men were too weary to go, so they stayed behind. David and four hundred of his men pursued the Amalekites and recovered everything and took all the flock and herd the Amalekites had. So when it came time to divide the spoil, some of David's four hundred men said the two hundred who were weary shouldn't get anything because they didn't work for it. For that moment their greed blinded them to see every battle they fought with the two hundred and how the two hundred have always been faithful. The decision came down to David, and this is what David said, "My brethren, you shall not do so with what the Lord has given us, who has preserved us and delivered into our hand the troop that came against us. For who will heed you in this matter? But as his part is who goes down to the battle, so shall his part be who stays by the supplies; they shall share alike" (1 Samuel 30:23). David loved justice. He exercised justice. God put him and allowed him to enter seasons where this virtue will be purified and perfected before he steps into the height of his calling.

DELIGHTS IN THE PRESENCE OF GOD

This is huge for God. The king had to be a person who desired the presence of God. And David was a person who desired deeply to be in the presence of God. God had set David's life up so that His presence was the only thing that satisfied David and gave him joy. But most importantly David's delight in the presence of God was prophetic. His delight in the presence of God was bigger than him. There was something bigger than David taking place. Thus the requirement for his delight was also immense. Let me explain. God used David's time in the wilderness to reveal Himself to David. David nurtured his delight of the presence of God from his wilderness days. David developed a love for God's presence in solitude, in hiding places, and in caves. God took everything else from David so he could delight in His presence alone. God was preparing David for a prophetic delight for when he will be king.

In the Old Testament times, the presence of God also known as the arc of the covenant dwelled in the Tabernacle of Moses. The Tabernacle of Moses had three levels. The outer court, the inner court, and the Holy of Holies. God's presence also known as the arc of the covenant dwelt in the Holy of Holies. The closer you drew to the Holy of Holies, the more intense His presence was manifested. The only person who was allowed to enter the Holy of Holies was the high priest, and he would only enter to the Holy of Holies once a year for the atoning of sin. The regular people never entered the Holy of Holies. The tabernacle operated under strict restrictions. Things operated like this for a long time. When David became king, he made a trip to Gibeon to bring to Jerusalem the arc of the covenant. David moved the arc of the covenant. It was the object that carried the presence of God. It was the holy of holies. This is what David carried, and left behind the tabernacle of Moses. The arc of the covenant was transferred to David's tabernacle. The tabernacle of David was very different from the tabernacle of Moses. This tabernacle didn't have the three levels separating people from the presence of God like the tabernacle of Moses had. It only had the Holy of Holies and people had access to the presence of God. Freely. People made sacrifices of praise. Gentiles had access to the presence of God. People danced and shouted praises to God. This period lasted for a short while. When Solomon, David's son, built the temple, the priests took the arc of the covenant and placed it in the holy of holies. The restrictions were restored. And only the high priest could go into the Holy of Holies once a year.

From this point forth many prophets started prophesying about the return of the tabernacle of David. Prophets like Amos in Amos 9:11-12 and Isaiah in Isaiah 16:5. David's tabernacle didn't have any restrictions. People of all kind had access to the presence of God. This was foreshadowing the life of the believer after the resurrection of Chris Jesus. When Jesus died on the cross, the veil of the temple was torn in two. All the believers had access to the Holy of Holies. The author of Hebrews put it clearly when he said "Let us therefore come boldly to the throne of grace, that we may obtain mercy and find grace to help in time of need" (4:16).

David's delight for the presence of God was prophetic. God used David to display a prophetic delight in His presence that believers would have through faith in Christ Jesus. The psalms David wrote overflow with the delight for the presence of God that Christians have desired to have for centuries. The destiny of David was futuristic. God had to separate David from people so he could learn to enjoy His Presence. That he may be equipped to display what life would be like for the believer when the prophecy of the Messiah is fulfilled.

16

We don't get the memo

God sees the end of everything at the same time as He sees the beginning. That's why He is a full picture God. He saw David's end before the beginning and that's why He took David through the process He took him through to prepare him for what was ahead of him. God sees all the generations that will come through you and after you, that's how far He sees. Don't allow your shortsightedness to question His all-knowing nature. David had no idea that killing bears and lions was boot camp. He had no clue that killing Goliath was internship for the battles ahead. He didn't know that all the times he was alone it was a setup by God to push him to cultivate a deeper relationship with Him. He had no idea that he enrolled in crisis management classes when faced with the dilemma at Keilah and Ziklag. God didn't give David any notice concerning what was required of Him. He didn't brief David on his character development strategy as preparation for the royal office. David never got the memo. But David was obedient to the Lord. He had a functioning perspective. He was obedient to the ways and the Word of God.

As I said before, your destiny is what determines your character requirement. Your character requirement is what determines the process where God develops your character. We all have different character requirements based on where God is calling us. Our processes are different because our destinies are different. God may be calling you to a prophetic destiny that speaks to the next seven generations. He may be calling you to impact a nation. But the truth remains. We don't get the memo. God doesn't issue memos on the process you will go through. You don't receive a text when you wake up saying, "Get ready, this is what's coming for you today, seize it when it shows up." We don't have this luxury.

But God does communicate, just not in the way we expect to receive such information. Below are His versions of memos.

The memo is the opportunity for growth in front of you right now. The memo is the opportunity to serve in front of you right now. The memo is the obstacle and challenge you need to overcome in your life right now. The memo is the fear you need to conquer in your life right now. The memo is the difficult situation you are in right now where obeying God will cost you something. The memo is the opportunity for God to get the glory through the impossible you're facing right now. Seize it.

Cry out to God like the psalmist who said, "Search me, God, and know my heart; test me and know my anxious thoughts. See if there is any offensive way in me, and lead me in the way everlasting" (Psalm 139:23-24, NIV).

Take time to introspect so you can recognize the areas of growth you need to work on. What areas of your character has God revealed to you that you need to work on? Don't prolong your process. Get on it. Work on it. He is at work.

THE OPPORTUNIST

In your process God will allow the hardest tests to come your way so your character can be purified. In the darkest hour of David's journey to the throne he was presented with a way out. Saul and his guards were sleeping fofofo. David managed to get to Saul. David's entourage encouraged David to kill Saul to end their days on the run. But David refused. Instead, he obeyed God by not touching his anointed. At the same time displaying mercy and grace. David seized the opportunity. He passed the test. And for the first time Saul publicly endorses David as the next king. He endorsed him in front of his army of three thousand and in front of David and his men. It was now official. David will be king. This was by far the hardest test for David at that point in his life. But David seized it.

As a believer of Christ Jesus, you need to be an opportunist. Always looking for an opportunity to grow, to serve, to seek the Lord, to honor God, to glorify the Lord, to strengthen your trust in God, to persevere and to be like Christ.

Like an intern who wants to get the job

Like a rookie who wants to be a champion

Like an artist who wants to create a masterpiece

Like a team that wants the championship

The opportunists seize the process. A Christian opportunist is not selfish but she or he is selfless. Their biggest goal and desire is to be like Christ. Any opportunity that gets them closer to this, they seize. Any opportunity that pushes them further from this, they leave. David was an opportunist. That's why when bears and lions came, David went after them and he killed them.

When Goliath was defying the armies of Israel, he saw this as an opportunity and he seized it.

God is taking you through different seasons within your process to teach you different things. To equip you, develop you, build you and prepare you. Are you seizing the opportunities or are you running from them? Playing around and wasting opportunities every day?

Are you seizing an opportunity to love?

Are you seizing an opportunity to forgive?

Are you seizing an opportunity to be brave?

Are you seizing an opportunity to be humble?

Are you seizing an opportunity to exercise faith?

Are you seizing an opportunity to glorify God?

Are you seizing an opportunity to be faithful?

Are you seizing an opportunity to persevere?

Your victory predates you. It was released long before you were born. Will you seize it? Or will you allow the enemy to continue taunting and mocking you? The memo comes in a form of an opportunity. Seize it.

Being an opportunist is not about making things work for you. It's about rewarding God for choosing to trust you with the opportunity. God trusts you, so seize every opportunity you can to show that He is true when he says, nothing He allows to come your way is too big for you. Seize opportunities to display that you trust Him.

HEART OF A SERVANT

Most people who talk about David never miss the fact that he was a servant. I am not going to miss it either. When you look at the life of David from the days of living in his father's house to when he was crowned king, the attitude of his heart was that of a servant. He was first and foremost a servant of God, but it didn't end here for David. He also served those who were around him. When he was living in his father's house David was serving his father by tending sheep and running house errands. When the royal office hired him, he was serving Saul in different ways, from playing slow jams for him to fighting next to him as his armor bearer in battle. It's easy to think this was easy, I mean David served as a musician to Saul but also as his soldier. He was summoned by Saul to come and play music for him when he was a national hero, and David never said, "ain't nobody got time for that." David was not interested in getting ahead of everybody else by being leader over everyone else. David got ahead of everyone else because he outserved everyone else. Are you a servant? Do you serve those above you? Do you serve those below you? Serving is both ways, upward and downward. Are you serving the people God has put in your life? Are you serving the leaders God has put in your life? Are you serving those God has put in your care? Be it your boss, your parents, your pastor, your family, your employees, your government, your friends? Being a servant is an attitude one embodies deep within them, the outworking of this attitude is stewardship.

17

Faithful stewardship

Stewardship is the currency for elevation. When you are faithful with a little you will be faithful with more. Stewardship plays a huge role in your process. When you are a steward it means there is an owner you are accountable to. We are first and foremost accountable to God before we are to anyone else. In the context of the process we are stewards of God's grace. But we won't focus on this. We will look into two kinds of stewardship. First is stewardship of gifts and talents and the second is the stewardship of current assignments.

STEWARDSHIP OF GIFTS AND TALENTS

David was a gifted worshipper (music). He trained to play the harp as a child probably while tending sheep in the wilderness. He was so good at it, that people knew him for his musical craftsmanship. He wasn't a superstar. He didn't have platinum records. He didn't have a number 1 record on the charts. He didn't have sold out shows. But he was faithful to his gift. He practiced and practiced to the point he was so good that when the king needed a skilled player to calm him down, David's name came up. The faithful stewardship for his gift got him to perform for the king. If David was a horrible player, that opportunity would've gone to someone else. But he was faithful to his gift and he was the best at what he did. When God opened the door and the opportunity came to him, he was prepared and ready. David was called and anointed to be a king but what got him to the palace is his musical gift. You don't know how far your gift will take you. Be faithful, it could be the thing that opens the door to your destiny.

David was also a gifted fighter. While his brothers went to Saul's military academy he was tending sheep. But this didn't stop him from training. He learned military strategy in the wilderness battling lions and bears. David had perfected the art of sling shooting. He tirelessly trained in this art. He was the best. The sling was like a machine gun to David. And he was a sharp shooter. Bears and lions died from his shots. He was a pro. And this led him to victory. If David was a lousy and lazy sling shooter, he definitely would've been the one dead that day on the valley of Elah. But his faithfulness to his gift of military strategy led him to defeating Goliath. This moment of victory changed his whole life.

God has given you a gift. You might be gifted in music, writing, photography, science, sports, preaching, teaching, designing, agriculture, business, technology engineering etc. Are you being faithful to your gift at the moment? What are you doing daily to perfect and maximize your gift? How are you getting better at your talent and gift? It's all about stewardship. The release of your miracle depends on God. But the experience of your miracle depends on your stewardship. God can't present to you a book publishing deal if you're an awful writer, you'll embarrass yourself. God can't present to you a major business opportunity if you don't have the resources and capacity to do it in a way that would glorify Him. God won't give you something you're not ready for.

Most of us want the opportunity before we start working on our talent and gift. We want to see the opportunity presented to us before we get ready for it. But you won't seize an opportunity you aren't prepared for. David didn't know that he would face Goliath. He was just being faithful to his gift of sling shooting and battle strategy. You need to measure your faithfulness over your gift every day. If you're an athlete, train. If you're a writer, write. If you're a filmmaker, make films. If you're a scholar, study. If you're a farmer, farm. If you're a tech engineer, develop solutions. If you're a counselor, counsel people. Be the best. This is how you go from glory to glory. Stewardship is about doing and growing. Be a faithful steward over what God has gifted you in.

STEWARDSHIP OF CURRENT ASSIGNMENTS

We have all been assigned to something. Right now you are assigned to do something. It could be your job, your ministry, your family, your studies, a project, a tender, or a gig. We are all assigned to something. David was faithful at every assignment he was given. When he was a shepherd boy, he was a faithful shepherd. He gave it all he had. He didn't hold back. He didn't treat it as a transition; he did it like it was everything he would ever do. We see the level of his faithfulness and commitment when he attacks the lion and the bear that try to eat his sheep. This got him a reputation for being a mighty man of valor. In fact, David's experience as a shepherd is what gave him an added advantage against Saul in the wilderness. In Saul's own words, David was known to be crafty. He knew his way around the wilderness. They couldn't catch him. He knew how to navigate the wilderness. He was well acquainted with the wilderness in his days tending sheep. Your current assignment has tremendous value to your future tribulation, assignment and blessing. If David was a mediocre shepherd, he probably would've been caught in the wilderness. Don't get me wrong. Yes, God did His part but for what God had released to manifest, David had to be prepared and equipped to unleash. David did his part. He was the best at whatever he did. He was faithful at every door the Lord opened for him. Whether it's tending sheep or leading 1,000 soldiers. His good stewardship of current assignments is what propelled him to the next level. It's what took him from strength to strength, from glory to glory. It's what kept him alive.

Your current assignment is packed with so many layers of victory and preparation. Seize it. Own it. Be the best at it. Your current assignment matters more than you know. Be faithful. Your future depends on it.

David's next job was playing the harp in the palace. He did this with everything he had. He soothed the spirit of Saul. He was always there. He was consistent and faithful at his job. After this, he was promoted to be a commander over one thousand soldiers. And even on this level he kept slaying. He was so faithful that the Bible says, "David behaved wisely in all his ways..." (1 Samuel 18:14) and in another part it says, "David behaved more wisely than all the servants of Saul..." (1 Samuel 18:30). Behaving wisely is biblical for "to act with high level skills" David gave his current assignment as a commander everything he had. He acted with high-level skill in all his ways. He acted with skill better than everyone else. He was the best at whatever he was commanded to do. He was once again the best at what he did. David was faithful at all his assignments whether mundane or glorious.

Faithful stewardship is paramount. It propels you to your destiny. Are you faithfully stewarding the assignment you currently have been graced to have? The problem with the majority of Christians is that we want to get to our destinies so badly that we neglect our current assignments, thus jeopardizing our process and damaging our destinies.

In your process you will sometimes find yourself in unfamiliar and unpleasant assignments. But you have to be a faithful steward of that assignment. Joseph never planned to be a slave worker, but he was faithful at his job. He never planned to be a supervisor in prison while he is also a prisoner, but he was faithful at his assignment. God elevates those who faithfully steward their gifts and current assignments. When you are not a faithful steward, you make God look like an unfaithful God.

THE VIRUS

David was not perfect. He was a human being like the rest of us. He made horrible mistakes, which cost him a lot. David was very faithful in his process but there's one area where he was unfaithful. Women. David didn't obey God's command for one wife. He tolerated this issue and it infected his soul leading up to the moment he saw Bathsheba. His soul was numb to the sin. But this sin started when young David was on the run. It started when he was in his process to become king.

When David was on the run, Saul married David's wife Michal to someone else. She would later become David's wife again. But for a while David was an unofficially divorced fugitive. As an unofficially divorced fugitive and a hero on the run, David encounters Abigail, the wife of Nabal. This story is found in 1 Samuel 25.

This is the backstory of their meeting. Nabal's servants had been tending sheep in the wilderness and they came across David and his men. This was the season of sheep shearing, so sheep were like gold to thieves. David and his men protected Nabal's flock and his servants. And because of the wonderful security service David provided to Nabal, he sent word to Nabal saying he needs to be compensated. He didn't name his price but he was good with whatever Nabal saw fit. When word got to Nabal, he pretended to have no knowledge of who David is. He also reviled David. When David got this feed-back, he got angry and decided to go and kill the entire house of Nabal. Now when news of what Nabal did reached his wife, the wife decided to go plead with David. The Bible describes Abigail as a woman of good understanding and beautiful appearance. You know, the kind that David likes. When Abi-gail pleads with David, David extends mercy and gives his word to Abigail that he won't kill anyone. Abigail goes back home; she tells her husband what happened.

After hearing what happened, Nabal gets a stroke and dies instantly. Da-vid and his fugees shed no blood. Ready or not, they never came. And Nabal wasn't killed soft either. Shortly afterwards David swoops in and proposes to Abigail. Abigail says yes, and she becomes his wife. As if this replacement for Michal is not enough, David marries another girl called Ahinoam. David is a fugee on the run, his life is in danger and a brother has three wives already.

The love for women was the virus that ate David and his destiny. This vi-rus grew to a point where David slept with the wife of one of his mighty men. Uriah risked his life to protect David's life when Saul wanted to kill him. David was so numb that he killed Uriah just to protect himself from shame. This obscene behavior didn't start when he saw Bathsheba. It started when David was in his process as a young man. He tolerated this sin and it led to his fall. Because of this, God cursed his descendants. He divided his kingdom. The divided kingdom fought a lot. The northern kingdom was eventually eliminated from the face of the earth by Assyria. This is how badly the virus can jeopardize and destroy you and your destiny.

What sin are you tolerating in your process? What issue are you ignoring in your process? What weakness are you trying to burry in your process? You need to deal with it right now. It is a virus. It will slowly infect your entire being. If you don't deal with it now, it's going to lead you to your demise. You can't compromise. You need to be vigilant about it. You need to be intentional about it. Stop thinking you will be the exception. You won't.

Paul wrote, "Now all these things happened to them as examples, and they were written for our admonition, on whom the ends of the ages have come" (1 Corinthian 10:11). He was talking about how the Old Testament stories were written as firm warnings to us. In the Old Testament we see where Saul's disobedience led. We see that tolerating sin not only destroys you but a hundred or a thousand others the way David's sin did. We see how deception will only hold you back, the way it held Jacob back. We see how idolatry leads to destruction, the way it did for the Israelites.

There's a popular saying: "learn from the mistakes of others." This saying is truer of the biblical stories that are written for our admonition. We saw how David's faithfulness in the process led to tremendous victory. We have seen how his faithfulness in the process led to David glorifying God on the throne. But we have also seen how his unfaithfulness and tolerance of sin in the process led to his demise. We will never know the fullness of David's destiny because the virus ate it up. Let's learn from David. Let us live to see the fullness of our destinies in our time. Don't compromise in your process. That compromise will be your downfall.

CLOSE THE CASTING

Your life is a big picture story. It transcends beyond your generation. Its impact will touch people's lives for many generations to come, for eternity. But your life needs a director. It needs a leader. And the leader can't be you. You don't know your destiny. You don't know what you will face tomorrow. You don't know how many lives you will touch. But there is the One who is qualified for the role. The One who will turn your big picture story into an epic tale that rewards Christ for His suffering and glorifies Him with every inch of your being. This is the kind of tale I want my life to tell. This is the kind of epic story I want your life to tell. Will you choose Him to direct your big picture story? Will you enter into a covenant of faith with Him? Will you submit to Him?

David's life was a big picture story much like yours. David's destiny was so colossal there is no way he could've reached there without walking with God, the way Enoch did. There is no way he could've reached there without being faithful in the process. There is no way he could've reached there without having a functioning perspective. There is no way he could've reached there without being conformed to the image of God. After all, he was a man after God's own heart. When David was king, these were the words of God to David through prophet Nathan, "Now therefore, thus shall you say to My servant David, 'Thus says the Lord of hosts" I took you from the sheepfold, from following the sheep, to be ruler over My people, over Israel. And I have been with you wherever you have gone, and I have cut off all your enemies from before you, and I have made you a great name, like the name of the great men who are on earth" (2 Samuel 7:8-9).

God was directing the story of David from day one. David submitted himself into God's direction. And the rest of his life is history. Are you closing down the casting? Or are you still looking for someone else to direct your big picture story? What's it going to be? Who is it going to be?

the greatest job of all time **the greatest job of all time** *the greatest job of all time* ***the greatest job of all time*** *the greatest job of all time* ***the greatest job of all time*** *the greatest job of all time* ***the greatest job of all time*** *the greatest job of all time* **the greatest job of all time** *the greatest job of all time* ***the greatest job of all time*** *the greatest job of all time* **the greatest job of all time** *the greatest job o*

Rewarding the suffering of the slain lamb

18

Mission focused ambition

I was hanging out with friends one evening. And one of them, a pastor, said something that is common knowledge yet nonetheless interesting. He said, "there are very few born again Christians, fewer than we think there are." Upon hearing this I subconsciously thought, this is not new information. But then he took it further; he said we think there are a lot of Christians because we are around other Christians. Especially if you are a Christian who is committed to a local church and you have a church family, whether it is through the ministry you serve under or the small groups.

This sort of environment and atmosphere is wonderful; it helps us grow and it also keeps us safe from the lies of the world. But it also poses a danger. It makes the need for evangelism less tangible. Because in Christian circles salvation is not the need, sanctification is. And we focus on becoming like Christ and forget why Christ died and rose again.

When we are in the process, we become too consumed by our hustle.

We become too involved by our callings and dreams. Our focus becomes the breakthrough we are waiting for, while sinners are perishing every day. Consumed by our hustle and process, we forget that Christ died to save sinners. That the death and resurrection of Christ is the reason we are still here on earth. And our utmost priority should be rewarding His suffering. We reward His suffering by sharing the gospel, winning lost souls and making disciples.

In the process, you meet God's utmost desire, worship

In the process, you become what God desires, Christ-like

In the process, you bring Him what He is worthy of, Glory

In the process, you experience what God desires for you, full joy.

In the process, you develop an utmost desire, the pursuit of God

In the process, you partake in the highest honor, rewarding His suffering

When we are in the process, we need to see beyond our peripheral. We need to see beyond our destiny. We need to see beyond our breakthrough. We need to see beyond our dreams. We need to see beyond our calling. We need to see eternity. The sight of eternity will illuminate the state of the world.

THE STATE OF THE WORLD

The world is living under an extreme state of sin. Some of which is legalized. The world has thought God away. People are living their lives as if they are not accountable to God. To them, God is dead. And if He is alive, then He is a mean and an unfair God. The world is in an atrocious state.

But the Word says, "For God so loved the world that He gave His only begotten Son, that whoever believes in Him should not perish but have everlasting life" (John 3:16). God's response to the dire state of the world was to sacrifice His son, so we can have life. Our response to the vile state of the world is to reward Christ's suffering by inviting sinners into a relationship with Him. The mission we are called into is not about making the world a better place. It is about rewarding Christ for His sacrificial love for the world. Thus making the world a Godly place.

We will all stand before our loving God one day to give an account for our lives. This day both excites me and terrifies me. I am excited because God has said that nothing we do for His kingdom is ever useless, He recognizes it and He will reward it. I am terrified because Jesus will judge us in an area many of us fall short, obeying His parting command.

HIS PARTING COMMAND

In the process, you need to honor the parting command by Jesus. When Jesus was about to ascend to Heaven, His last Words to His followers were, "But you shall receive power when the Holy Spirit has come upon you; and you shall be witnesses to Me in Jerusalem, and in all Judea and Samaria, and to the end of the earth" (Acts 1:8). He also said "Go therefore and make disciples of all the nations, baptizing them in the name of the Father and of the Son and of the Holy Spirit, teaching them to observe all things that I have commanded you; and lo, I am with you always, *even* to the end of the age" (Matthew 28:19-20).

This was Jesus's parting command. We know this as the great commission. In your process you need not forget His parting command. You will go through different processes in your life. These seasons will come and go but His parting command will remain regardless of your season. We need to honor His parting command. We need to be mission-focused people. We need to develop mission-focused ambitions.

MISSION FOCUSED AMBITION

God wants to take you from having self-focused ambitions to having mission-focused ambitions. He wants to take you from self-fulfilling dreams to mission-fulfilling dreams. God is using the process to break you to a point where you are filled with love and agony for the lost but even more for His sacrifice on the cross. And moving you past sentimental feelings to a point where your calling and your dreams partake in the great harvest of lost souls. Whether you are a mom or a farmer, a pastor, a doctor, an engineer, an artist, an administrator or a billionaire, your ambitions need to revolve around the great commission.

How is your calling and dream partaking in the great commission? This is the highest calling we have all been called to. In your process right now, how are you partaking in the great commission? How are you reaching out to those around you?

When you realize you don't own anything in this world, you handle the things in your "possession" differently. When you realize you are simply a steward of all that you have and dream of, you will live differently. The time you have is not yours, it's God's, and you are simply a steward of it. The dreams you have aren't yours, they are God's, and you are simply a steward of those dreams.

When you plant an apple tree and it produces fruit, both the apple tree, the fruit and the seed inside the fruit are yours. God creates us, so both our self, and all we dream and create, belongs to Him. We don't have ownership of anything. This is where accountability comes in. Stewardship creates accountability. We steward that which belongs to someone else. We are accountable to the One who owns that which we steward. Our capacity to dream and create belongs to God and so does everything that flows from this ability. Abusing this ability is mocking God. Millions of people today abuse this ability; their dreams don't exalt God nor do they partake in the great commission. Their creative energy serves self instead of serving the One they will answer to.

Your ambition needs to be harvest (lost souls) focused. Your process needs to be harvest focused. Come to think of it, as long as it is called today, the harvest of lost souls needs to be your focus. We are called to partake in building an army of believers.

BUILDING AN ARMY OF BELIEVERS

Nothing illustrates the kingdom of heaven better than this parable by Jesus in Matthew 13:31-32:

"The kingdom of heaven is like a mustard seed, which a man took and sowed in his field, which indeed is the least of all seeds; but when it is grown it is greater than the herbs and becomes a tree, so that the birds of the air come and nest in its branches."

The kingdom of God is the body of Christ, the church. The church grows fast because we are designed to work together, much like the human body. We play different roles, we have complimentary gifts and we have complimentary ministries. They form and create harmony that fosters the church growth. The Holy Spirit is the Person that gives life in all these harmonies and means for growth. Without Him there is no church.

The growth of the church happens when sinners turn to Christ. This is the first step in the circle of evangelism. The next phase is discipleship, and the circle is complete when those disciples are making disciples. This is the point of evangelism. Jesus commissioned us to make disciples. A disciple is a devoted follower of Christ. S/he is a person who is producing other disciples.

We can't subdue the world without reaching the lost. The more disciples there are, the more diversity we have as the body of Christ. The more diverse we are, the more we are able to reach other people. There are people you will never reach even if you become a billionaire and preach in sold out world arenas, but your unsaved friend, colleague, relative and the guy sitting next to you can reach those people.

There is an urgency to reach the lost. We are in the end times. Don't wait till the manifestation of your dreams, breakthroughs and calling before you spread the gospel. We need to go to work now. For God so loved the world that He gave. What are you giving to the harvest in your process? God loves His people and He wants to save them from eternal damnation and give them life. People are suffering every day because they don't know that there is a God who loves them unconditionally.

I once heard a phrase, "take care of God's business and He'll take care of your business." I don't want you to go into this with this mindset. You are not cutting a deal with God. You will preach the gospel because Christ loves the world and He died for it. Christ deserves the reward for His suffering. You will prioritize the harvest in your process not because you are cutting a deal with God. You know; the one for you God and one for me kind of deal, NO! You will prioritize the harvest because it is God's priority. Because God's heart is aching for the lost souls, He loves the sinners so much and He wants to be in a relationship with them.

LIVING SACRIFICE

In your process you will go through different seasons. Some will be breezy and some full of trials. How you live through these seasons will testify of the God you believe in. Paul exhorts believers to offer their bodies as living sacrifices in his letter to the Romans.

"I beseech you therefore, brethren, by the mercies of God that you present your bodies a living sacrifices, holy, acceptable to God, which is your reasonable service" (Romans 12:1).

This act of offering your body as a living sacrifice does more than glorify God through your life; it displays God to the world around you. How is your life in the process a testimony to those around you? Most of us think we will have enough credibility to testify about Christ when we've experienced the breakthrough, when our dreams come true and when we are living out our calling. But that is not as powerful as the world seeing you have peace in the midst of confusion in your process. It's not as powerful as them seeing you with joy in the midst of trials and pain. This is the powerful testimony. In your process, you need to learn to be vulnerable and let people see the pain and confusion you are in and how God is carrying you through it. This is the testimony the world is groaning to hear. Use this testimony to invite those who don't believe in Christ into a relationship with the Lord. You need to learn to be a spinner. Spinning conversations and turning them back to Calvary. Spinning your testimony back to Calvary. Spinning people's tragedies back to Calvary.

In the process, you meet God's utmost desire, worship

In the process, you become what God desires, Christ-like

In the process, you bring Him what He is worthy of, Glory

In the process, you experience what God desires for you, full joy.

In the process, you develop an utmost desire, the pursuit of God

In the process, you partake in the highest honor, rewarding His suffering

In the process, you get to be the living sacrifice that testifies of the ultimate sacrifice

ALL AUTHORITY

How do you respond when a Person with ALL authority both in heaven and on earth gives you an order? To be honest with you for a long time I have been responding to Jesus as if He had lesser authority, as if His jurisdiction is only in Heaven and as long as we are here on earth it's my turf. But the Word of God puts me in my place; "Jesus came and spoke to them, saying, "All authority has been given to Me in heaven and on earth" (Matthew 28:18). I believe this is huge. He says all authority, not some, not most, not just, but all. This means no government, no peoples, no principality, no kingdom; no one both in Heaven and on earth has higher authority than Him. The order He gives, no one can overrule. The righteous and just judgment He makes no one can overrule. And His dominion cannot be overthrown.

Out of all the times Jesus could've said this, He chose this moment. Using these words to set the stage for what He was going to say next. He knew that what He was about to say next was not easy, it would cost those who follow Him their freedom, their comfort, their lives, their safety, their dignity, their families, their friends, their status, and so much more. Jesus then said, "Go therefore and make disciples of all nations, baptizing them in the name of the Father and of the Son and of the Holy Spirit, "teaching them to observe all things that I have commanded you; and lo, I am with you always, even to the end of the age" (Matthew 28:19-20).

The command to make disciples of all nations is preceded by Jesus revealing the authority He has. I love the order of His speech here. There is something profound and powerful. Jesus says He has all authority on earth; this means only He will keep us accountable to the command He gave us. His authority overrules every other authority that tries to prohibit His disciples from making other disciples. This means we can't fear or tremble from the threats and penalties of lesser authorities that prohibit the great commission. His authority overrules every other authority. This means at the end of time when we stand before Him for judgment, we won't have admissible excuses. We can't say, "Ooh Jesus, my boss said I shouldn't preach" or "My government considered preaching the gospel an offense worthy of the death penalty Lord!" or "Jesus, in my time, it just wasn't cool to preach the gospel, I mean it was considered ancient and very Jehovah witness." or "Jesus, I just never had the courage to do it and I honestly missed this part where you have all the authority, I mean if I knew this I definitely would've done it." There won't be any excuse that will be admissible on this day. Because any excuse will be overruling His authority. And His authority cannot be overruled.

He also says He has all authority in heaven. This means He has the power and authority to honor in heaven those who honor His authority here on earth. Those who are faithful to His command will be rewarded and those who aren't will suffer loss.

The one with all authority both in Heaven and on earth is the one who is sending you to make disciples. You don't answer to anybody else but Him. No authority is higher than His. He is not sending you from a place of need. He is sending you from a point of authority.

FROM 120 to BILLIONS

The disciples had been trained for three years but they didn't have the power yet. Jesus then tells them, "But you shall receive power when the Holy Spirit has come upon you; and you shall be witnesses to Me in Jerusalem, and in all Judea and Samaria, and to the end of the earth" (Acts 1:8). He was addressing a group of five hundred disciples, but only one hundred and twenty were waiting for the Holy Spirit in the upper room. The Holy Spirit fell upon them on the day of Pentecost. It was only one hundred and twenty disciples who were equipped to be witnesses of Jesus in all Jerusalem, and in all Judea and Samaria, and to the rest of the world. And from that day billions of people have received Christ. To think it all started with a group of one hundred and twenty Holy Spirit empowered disciples is just mind-blowing. This group has rewarded the suffering of Christ more than any other group ever will.

This group reveals the potential of Holy Spirit empowered Christians who are fully submitted to reward Christ for His suffering. They are un-stoppable. But I think to myself, if this group of one hundred and twenty is watching us today, what are they thinking? What are they seeing? I mean, we are so much more than they were, and aside from the Holy Spirit, we have far more than they had. We have better conditions than they had, we have a complete Bible, we have hundreds if not thousands of evangelism resources, most of us have way less hostile environments to preach the gospel, we have better resources than they ever dreamed they could have and we have far more advanced infrastructure than they had. Yet it seems we are doing less than they did.

When I look at the one hundred and twenty disciples, I see you reaching your entire world and beyond. When I look at the one hundred and twenty disciples, I see a local church reaching an entire city. When I look at them, I see the church reaching an entire nation. When I look at them, I see the church reaching an entire continent. When I look at this group, I see the church reaching every person in the entire world. They went from one hundred and twenty to billions. We can go from millions to every person in the world.

PRIVACY WORSHIPERS

As I mentioned before, the hustle usually consumes you when you are in the process. You become occupied with your destiny and you become occupied with you. No words describe one of the major obstacles for preaching the gospel and discipleship better than what Francis Chan coined "privacy worshippers." We are so consumed by our own lives, our families, our friends, our quality time and we forget that people are perishing eternally every day. I am guilty of this. But don't get me wrong, I am not against privacy, I am quite a private person myself, but being private is one thing and worshiping privacy is another. Being private is one thing and using privacy as a shield against preaching the gospel and discipling others is another thing. We can't be private at the expense of compassion. We can't be private at the expense of someone's eternal destiny.

In the process, we need to open up our lives, our time and our homes so people can hear about Christ Jesus. Nothing is more honorable and rewarding than rewarding the suffering of the slain lamb. We need to do this now for we know not the hour. We need to become all-nighters.

ALL NIGHTERS

Every new day carries the possibility of being the second coming of Christ. Every brand new day shelters the possibility of being your last day on earth. This is our reality. This is your reality. This reality is not meant to instill fear in you but rather instill a strong desire to seize opportunities before it's too late. The Word of God says, "Watch therefore, for you know neither the day nor the hour in which the Son of Man is coming" (Matthew 25:13).

Living our lives as a people who are ready for Christ's return at any moment disconnects us from this world. And this is the reason most of us don't want to take Jesus at His Word. We know how much it's going to cost us. We know the sacrifices we will need to make. As exciting and as attractive as eternity sounds, most of us are still hesitant to pay the price in this current life that will ensure rewards in the life to come. While Jesus is calling us to be all-nighters, we are sleeping and snoring.

But it's time to wake up. Jesus will return. And when He does, your problem will be what you did with the time He gave you and not the time you never had. It's time we stop living as if we know when He will come back or when we will fall dead. We need to stop living as if we have this advantage. We don't. We can die any second. While this is a great thing, after all, to be absent with the body is to be present with the Lord, the point here is not the security of your salvation and where you will spend your eternity, but rather how are you living for Christ in this age, in this world, in this time? You will never get this time back. You will never live in this world the way you do now. This is it. How are you rewarding Christ for His suffering in this present time? How are you doing this knowing He might return anytime?

In your process, you need to reward Christ for His suffering. This is why He died. He died so somebody else could have the gift of being in a relationship with Him. So that everyone can get the privilege to walk through his or her process with Christ Jesus. Without Christ, everything is pointless because it will all perish. The blood, sweat and tears people invest, all mean nothing if they don't have a relationship with Jesus. Without Christ there is no life. When you share Christ with someone else, you are sharing life with that person. That person will literary be eternally grateful to you. But more importantly, Jesus will be rewarded for His choice to love us and die for us. Share life with people in your process. No other task is more honorable in life than this.

Epilogue

Paul used the human body to give an illustration of the church. The church is the body of Christ. Christ is the head of this body of believers. Each organ plays a vital role in this body and no part is inferior to the other. Every person in the body of Christ plays a vital role and no one is inferior to another. We all matter as people and we all matter as participants in the call to build the body of believers, both the global church and the local church. You are called to be a laborer in God's harvest and in the work of subduing the earth. You are not inferior. Your role matters a lot. It matters not because of who you are but because of who is inside you. The One who is inside you is all-powerful, all knowing and ever sovereign. Inside you dwells the Spirit of God. You carry the presence and power of God inside you. And His power is what is needed to build the church. God is able to do immeasurably more than what we can ask or imagine, and He does it through the power of His Spirit that dwells and works in you.

THE COMMUNITY WE ARE CALLED TO BUILD

The community of believers is where every human being ought to desire to belong. Because this is a community grounded in love and unity. This is a community where the billionaire and the teacher are one family. This is a community where no one is superior to the other. In this community, we are all equal because the blood of the same Christ Jesus saved us all. There is authority in this community but authority doesn't mean superiority. It means servanthood. We delight in serving one another. People enter this community and they experience Christ. They experience love. They experience unity and equality. This is a community where we encourage one another, we uplift one another, we empower one another, we work together and we seek God together. We help and empower the poor and the oppressed. We heal the sick and deliver those in bondage. This is a community that is supposed to birth new trends, innovate, pioneer; a community that's always ahead of its time. A community that creates a Christ exalting atmosphere in the workplace, the gym, the mall, the radio, the office, the TV, the book stores, online, the playground, the clothing stores, the airplane, the hospital and in the schools. This is the community we are called to build. A community where a person walks into church when they walk into your store, your business, your blog, your gym, your office, your home, your hotel and so forth. People walk into church when they listen to your music, watch your shows and films, read your books. This community builds the church outside the local church. This is what we are called to be.

THE POWER OF THIS COMMUNITY

This community has the power, influence and capacity to disciple nations and shape culture. The power of this community lies in the manifest presence of the God in it. The move of God in this community is strong and it is unstoppable. This community has the power and capacity to preach the gospel to every creature, to disciple nations, to change government policies, to influence business practices, to preserve the moral decay of the world. To solve world problems: both the third world and the first world. To help those in need, both great and small. Improving the living standard of people.

This community makes the will of God prevail here on earth as it is in heaven. This community makes the glory of God shine so bright in this world. The works of this community are so abundant that the world marvels and glorifies God.

THE POWER OF YOUR PARTICIPATION

This community requires your participation, not your spectating. Your participation is powerful. Your participation is life changing. Your participation is one of a kind. God wants to do earth shattering things through you so He can get the glory. Don't quench Him.

There are two ends of the spectrum for people who spectate. One end is a group of people who think they are unworthy. This group is made to believe that their skills, gifts and talents and experience are of no value to the body of Christ. The second end of the spectrum is a group of people who believe they were created for the top spot so they don't want to serve.

To the first group, I want to tell you that your participation in building the church and subduing the earth is of great significance. To the second group, the kingdom of God operates very differently; it's all about serving. Those who want to be at the top serve the most. Quit spectating. Start participating. There are no exceptions in participation.

There's a beautiful parable to explain this insanity. There is a country where everyone wants to be a president so bad and the country finally elects ten million presidents. It becomes the most dysfunctional country of all time. There's no one at the city council office, the MP's office, the 10-cell leader's office and at the minister's office because the whole nation is full of presidents.

In fact, lets go to the Bible for a clearer illustration. Paul compares the church to the body in the New Testament. Imagine an entire body made up of eyes. How will you walk? How will you carry things? How will you eat? How will you hear? How will you smell? How will you even be alive? Each one of us has a part to play. God is the one who decides what role you play. You were created the way you are for a specific role. Own it!

We are all called to participate. You are called to participate. The body of Christ hasn't been as strong as it should be because Christians have been spectators instead of participants and contributors. We participate in the world. We spectate in the church. No more. This is the era of participation in the church. Where would the church be if Martin Luther, John Wesley, Saint Augustine, A.W. Tozer, C.S. Lewis, Paul of tarsus, John Piper, Moses Kulola, Billy Graham and Christopher Mwakasege had decided to spectate instead of participate? Stop spectating. Start participating. Stop talking yourself out of this. Start dreaming.

THE DREAM THAT KEEPS ON GIVING

What do you ask for when you enter the throne room of the all-powerful God? What do you dream of when the fulfiller of your dreams is a God with no limitations? What is your reality when the God you call Father is able to turn impossible to possible?

You are created to thrive with possibility thinking. This possibility thinking is directly linked to your Father, Almighty God. Your perspective finds Him and with Him endless immeasurable possibilities are birthed. You don't dream based on your ability. You dream based on His unlimited sovereignty. You don't ask based on what you deserve. You ask based on what will glorify Him. You don't live for you. You live for Him. You were restored at the cross. It's time to dream as a restored person.

The world has never been more in a place where it groans for children of God to subdue it. It's decaying. And it needs bold dreamers who will believe

God for the impossible and expect from Him the immeasurably more. Quit living an ordinary life. Quit being content with what God has done in your life. Quit being consumed with what you can't do. And open yourself up to what God can do through you.

How big is your dream? Is it something that you can achieve on your own? Is it a dream that you can achieve within your lifetime? You need to dream bigger. You need to have dreams big enough that it takes more than four generations to fulfill it. You need a dream that keeps on being fulfilled even after your grandchildren are dead. You can't have a single generation dream while you are serving an eternal God. You need to dream multigenerational. You need to think multigenerational. You need to pray multigenerational. You have multigenerational potential.

DARE TO BE A WORLD CHANGER

Will your dream make the world a Godly place? The Word of God says, "Let your light so shine before men, that they may see your good works and glorify your Father in heaven" (Matthew 5:16). The context of this Word is living a life that glorifies God. But this Word is not limited to our conduct. It extends to our dreams too. You are the light of this world; will your dreams shine more light to the world? You are the salt of the earth; will your dreams help preserve the moral decay of this world? Are your dreams making the world a Godly place? We are called to be world changers so God can be glorified. We need to dream at this capacity; the capacity of changing the world.

The Word also says, "You are of God, little children, and have overcome them, because He who is in you is greater than he who is in the world" (1 John 4:4). Again, the context here talks about false prophets but it's not limited to that. The principle here is that He who is in you is greater than he who is in the world. Do you believe this? If he who is in the world can change it from bad to worse every day, He who is in us can work through us to change it from where it is to a place where it glorifies Him. Steve Jobs said, "The people who are crazy enough to think that they can change the world, are the ones who do." This statement is true of the human race. We are capable of changing this world. But it's not about changing this world for the sake of change. It's not about making the world a better place. It's about making the world a Godly place. This is what we are called to. This is where we need to partner with God. The followers of Christ who are crazy enough to believe God can work through them to change the world are the ones who live to testify of the majestic world changing glory of God. Will you dare to be a world changer? And live to see the world glorify God for what He has done through you?

VISION 4:34

Your life needs vision that will unleash you into your dreams and calling. To Apostle Paul, it was to know Christ and His mysteries. He considered everything in this life rubbish compared to knowing Christ (Philippians 3:8, NIV), and he wanted this for all peoples. He persevered everything because his vision was to know Christ and His mysteries and to preach among the gentiles the unsearchable riches of Christ.

I remember when I stumbled upon John 4:34. I had read this text many times before but this time the Holy Spirit illuminated something special out of the text. My whole life, I was looking for that one thing that will keep me going through anything. A vision that I will give everything I have to attain. And John 4:34 was my answer. The search was complete. I found what I was looking for. From that day my food has become to do the will of my Father. The verse says:

"Jesus said to them, "My food is to do the will of Him who sent Me, and to finish His work"

This is what pushes me every day. That is my motivation. This is my determination. This is what pushed me to finish writing this book. It's what will push me to write the next one and another one after that. It's what will push me to do all that God has put in my heart to do. John 4:34 has become the push I need when I am slow. It has become the strong WHY I need when I lose sight of why I do this. It has become my sense of nourishment. It has become my sense of accomplishment and fulfillment. It has become my sense of direction in life. It has become the tunnel of fire I use to test and purify every investment of time, energy and money I make in life.

What is the vision for your life? Without it you will perish as Solomon puts it in Proverbs 29:18. For Steven Furtick, it is the 23rd page of the book Fresh Wind, Fresh Fire by Jim Cymbala. For John Piper, it is Jonathan Edwards' sermon transcript. For Mark Batterson, it's 2 Samuel 23:20. What is the vision for your life? If you don't have one, you need to seek the face of God and create one. Vision is monumental. Vision is the genesis of a Christ glorifying and a Christ rewarding life.

THE CALL TO DIE EMPTY

You are called to die empty of everything God has created you to do and accomplish. You were put here on earth for a purpose and with a purpose. That purpose has eternal significance but that eternal significance is directly dependent upon the earthly fulfillment of that purpose. The time to live a life of purpose is now. There is a parable known as the parable of Minas in the gospel of Luke chapter 19. This parable talks about faithful stewardship of what you have been given. In this parable, we see a group of ten servants. To each was given one mina by their master to do business till he returns.

One thing that never occurred to me until now is that these servants had other responsibilities and things to do. The master was gone for a long time but they lived, they ate, they fed their families, which means they had other responsibilities that earned them a living. But these things didn't have any value that would qualify for reward when the master returns. He would only use what He gave them to measure how He will reward them. This is paramount. Christ is not going to reward you for what you generally do but for your faithfulness over what He has called you to do. What He has assigned you to do is what has eternal significance.

When the master returned, we see one servant who was over the top faithful and produced ten times more than what he was given. We also see another servant who made five times more than what he was given. And finally, we see the guy who buried the mina. At the return of his master, he had the same mina he was given when the master left. This parable is a picture of the return of Christ to judge and reign. Which servant are you going to be? Will Christ receive more from you than what He gave you? Or will he find what He gave you untouched? Will He find those dreams untouched? Will He find that ministry untouched? Will He find those ideas untouched? Will He find that calling unfulfilled?

We know that Christ rewards the faithful servants greatly for their faithfulness. And we know how the story of the unfaithful servant ends. You don't want to be that guy. You don't want to meet Christ with your talent buried. With your gift buried. With your ideas buried. With your ministry buried. With your innovation buried. With your projects buried. With your business buried. You don't want to meet Christ with what He gave you untouched. Be faithful over what God has given you. Maximize it. Finish what God has put in your heart. Finish what you are called to do. Be like Jesus who finished it all. Be like Paul who finished the race. A successful life is dying empty, not dying wealthy. Dying empty in this life means rising up wealthy in the life to come. It's time to chase your dreams. It's time to unleash yourself into your destiny. It's time to have audacious faith. It's time to stop wasting your life. It's time to live a purpose driven life. It's time to live a restored life.

THE OUTRO

Today can be the beginning of the rest of your life. Today has the potential to be the genesis of a life you were created to live. Today can be the day you start living the restored life and dream restored dreams. Here are my final Words to you!

The Word of God is as good to your life

As your obedience to its Omega and Alpha

This book is as good to your life

As your obedience to its revealed truth

Your process is as successful

As your faithfulness on every turn

God's power is as present in your life

As the roots of your faith in Him

What's it going to be?

Supernatural reality

Hangs in your choice to believe

And your submission to obey

Your call!!!

Acknowledgement

This book has literary taken the effort of a whole village to reach you, from writing it to publishing it. And I want to honor the community that has helped make this book a reality.

First and foremost, I want to thank my Lord and savior Jesus Christ for loving me, redeeming me, choosing me, anointing me and never forsaking me. As if this is not enough, He also gave me the honor of writing this book. I did this for His glory alone through His Holy Spirit that works in me.

I want to thank my parents. To dad, thank you for everything and proud to call you father. To Mom, thank you for believing in me when I had nothing to show for it and most importantly, for praying for me throughout the years. Thank you for sacrificing so much so I can have what I need to move forward. You are my hero. I love you mom, I love you pops. To my little sister Jacque, cling to your purpose girl, your faithfulness will impact many people. I love you kiddo.

To the one person who I know has been praying for me daily without fail, Bibi Mtende, thank you. I am blessed that you get to witness God's goodness to your lineage.

To my aunt and uncle Mr. & Mrs. Charles & Aneth Mapima, who invited me into their home and it's in this house where I heard the gospel night after night that served as seeds for later conviction. Thank you guys.

To my Sinza cell fellowship group, thank you for your prayers, encouragement, correction and exhortation.

I wouldn't be the man I am today if it wasn't for choosing to walk alongside a group of young men who are serious about pursuing God. I want to thank all of my Fearless Faith brothers and all the speakers who poured into us those legendary Friday nights.

To Pastor Jimmy Abrams, thank you for your leadership and the opportunities you've given me. To my Mama mdogo, Pastor Pam, thank you for believing in me and for giving me the opportunities to be uncomfortable and grow.

To Jun, thank you for your faithfulness week after week in designing artworks for what God is doing through me. I am honored that you got to design the cover of my first book.

To Alpha and Bitz, you guys are the dream team, thank you for always making yourselves available when I need to produce visual content. Your commitment to excellence is inspiring.

This book is a result of a lot of people sowing their money and resources into this dream. I want to thank Aidan Eyakuze, Benjamin Filskov, Johan De beer, Sigstance Mtui, Flavia, Victor Mwenda, Ford Maro, Karol Riwa, Paul Ndemanisho, Chris Jesuthasan, Chris Rwechungura, Happy Kikwa, Joshua Mlay, Ephy Musiba, Hopper Heaven, Godwin Msigwa, Isaiah Zachary, Don Kweka, Lusinda Nortje, Owden Godson, Edgar Lushaju, Franklin Kasumba, Adam Foya, David Boyd, Dr. Brenda Dmello, Eric Njumba, Isaac Donald, Christopher Bupe, Asta Hiza, David Karamagi, Sia Shayo, Peter Mpala, Josephine Mutahangarwa, Linda and Keir Teggisa, Juliet Kairuki, Frederick Sheshe and Gervas Lushaju. You guys are my heroes. I have mad respect for you. Thank you for believing in my dream. Thank you for being faithful stewards of God's grace.

Every successful man has a band of friends who stick closer than a brother. I am privileged to do life with a group of brothers called Super Conquerors. Chris, Paul, Ephy and Joshua, thank you for your prayers and support. We have had countless conversations about purpose and I am privileged to witness God's purpose for your lives unveil.

To the prayer team for this book, thank you guys. To Joyce, see your dreams through, sister! To Ephy, For His Sons & Daughters is only the beginning. To Joshua, on your knees is the right place to start. To Chris, Ombi will be the answer to the prayers of many. To Paul, a journey of a hundred thousand miles begins with a single step, keep stepping on brother.

I want to take this opportunity and recognize someone important and special to me, I want to thank my best friend in the whole world, Tina. You have been God's number one instrument in making me who I am today. You have tirelessly and selflessly wanted the best for me and I love you for it. You have talked me out of quitting and procrastination many times. God has used your gift of prophecy to encourage and edify me many times. You were the first one to see this moment and many other moments that are yet to happen, and you never held back on telling me what God is doing in me and through me. You have supported this book from day one with everything you have. You have helped and pushed me to give this book my very best by allowing God to say what He wants to say to His people. I am so excited to witness God edify and build His church through you. I appreciate you. I love you.

To everyone, God will reward you for the roles you play in making this book a success.

Abbreviations

AMP	AMPLIFIED BIBLE
AMPC	AMPLIFIED BIBLE, CLASSIC EDITION
ESV	ENGLISH STANDARD VERSION
KJV	KING JAMES VERSION
NIV	NEW INTERNATIONAL VERSION
NLT	NEW LIVING TRANSLATION
OT	OLD TESTAMENT

Notes

CHAPTER 1: CAN WE SKIP THIS PART?

Batterson, Mark. *Chase the Lion*. Colorado: Multnomah, 2016, pp. 201.

CHAPTER 3: THE RIGHT VIEW OF THE PROCESS

Pastor Cherish Crisp. http://allfearless.com/2012/09/the-mustard-seed-controversy/

CHAPTER 4: THE PROCESS AFFORDS US ULTIMATE WORSHIP

Steffany Gretzinger. https://www.youtube.com/watch?v=nNhI7vqMEoA .

Warren, Rick. *The Purpose Driven Life*. Michigan: Zondervan, 2002, pp. 68.

Hughes, Kent R. *Disciplines of a Godly Man*. Illinois: Crossway Books, 2001, pp. 111.

CHAPTER 6: MODELED FOR US AND COMMISSIONED TO US

Cornelius Tacitus, *The Annals*: New York. : Random House, Inc. 1942, pp

CHAPTER 7: A CHARACTER BUILT FOR IMPACT

Tozer, A. W. *The Pursuit of God*. Wisconsin: Aneko Press, pp. 16.

CHAPTER 8: CONFORMINTY TO CHRISTLIKENESS

Bevere, John. *Victory in the wilderness*. Colorado: Messenger Press, 1992, pp.71.

Batterson, Mark. *Chase the Lion*. Colorado: Multnomah, 2016, pp. 201.

Oxford Dictionary

CHAPTER 9: COMPLETE JOY FOR THE CHRISTLIKE

Study Bible (2nd Edition). Nashville: Thomas Nelson, 2007, 1690.

EPILOGUE: THE CALL TO SHAPE CULTURE

Steve Job. https://www.youtube.com/watch?v=8rwsuXHA7RA.

THANK YOU

FOR READING THIS BOOK

PLEASE HELP OTHERS CHOOSE
TO READ THIS BOOK BY RATING IT

AND REVIEWING IT.

CLICK THE QR CODE BELOW TO DO SO.

AGAIN, THANK YOU.